D1370765

Limes Are Yellow

Shopping for the Finest
at California's Farmers' Markets

Mary Luce Wellington

Illustrations by Ellen R. Bergstone

Sorrel Publishing
Santa Barbara, California

Printed in the United States of America

Cover and illustrations by Ellen R. Bergstone

Sorrel Publishing
P.O. Box 2492, Santa Barbara, CA 93118

Library of Congress Catalog Card Number 93-085385

      Wellington, Mary Luce
      Limes Are Yellow

ISBN 0-9637683-2-8 (pbk)

This book is dedicated to
my mother
who has encouraged my writing since I was a child.

CONTENTS

SECTION III VEGETABLES

ACKNOWLEDGMENTS

I could not have written this book without the help of a great many generous people.

Those growers who welcomed me to their farms are highlighted in the text and I would like to express my thanks to them. I want to thank all the other growers mentioned in the text who were generous with time and information.

Thanks go to the many market managers who were kind enough to respond to my correspondence and talk to me on the phone. They include: Lynn Bagley, *Marin*; Kamish Blume, *West Hollywood*; Roberta Childers, *Woodland*; Steve Christy, *Modesto*; Laura Dingle, *Santa Monica*; Steve Ginsburg, *Cloverdale*; Stacy Grecian, *Southland Farmers' Market Assoc.*; John Hensill, *Redwood City*; Richard Kane, *Castroville*; Marie Kendrat-Neubauer, *Contra Costa*; Laure Kendrick, *Carpinteria*; Wendy Krupnick, *Felton*; Melanie Mirez, *Venice*; Brigitte Moran, *San Rafael*; Rose Munoz, *Torrance*; Nevada County Certified Market Assoc.; Caroline Phillips, *Mountain View*; Sharon Seidenstein, *Berkeley*; Emi Tanioka, *Merced*; Mary Vienot, *San Francisco*; Doug Wolfe, *Red Bluff*; Richard Wood, *Potter Valley*.

I want to give special thanks to those who helped me in my efforts to present an accurate and understandable explanation of farming practices and food safety. Dr. Roberta Cook, Economist, UC Davis was invaluable help. Ron Gilman, Agricultural Commissioner of Santa Barbara County gave generously of his time as did Mary Ann Rajala, biologist with the Agricultural Commissioner's Office. Ron Labastida, president of the San Luis Obispo County chapter of the CCOF read my work and helped to assure accuracy.

I appreciate the feedback from customers when I displayed different cover designs and tossed out possible titles. Alice Pearce was a generous customer who became one of my proofreaders.

In addition to the research, experimenting, and writing that go into a book like this, there is a strong support system. I wish to give special thanks to my sister, Judith Reynolds; my mother, Gladness Luce; and friend, Barbie Graper, for their listening and encouragement and for their proof reading.

My son, Douglas, was my computer guru. I know how to turn on my computer and run the word processing program but he is the one who could listen to me over long distance telephone and know exactly what would come up on my screen and what to do with it when I had glitches. How I appreciated his cheerful patience!

NOTES

GENERAL INFORMATION

Chapter 1

WHY THIS BOOK

"We're moving to California!"

We were sitting in the living room of our fieldstone house on the bluff of Lake Erie. The living room had a large fieldstone fireplace and massive solid wood beams in the ceiling. An original gaslight still worked in the dining room. Very old ceramic tiles brought from Spain decorated the pulled plaster wall of the winding staircase. Secret passages and a tunnel took one from the library on the second floor to the detached garage outside. I loved this home.

My husband's pronouncement filled me with trepidation. It was, however, not completely unexpected. He was born and spent his first five years in Florida with yearly visits to the state thereafter. Palm trees, sand, and sunshine were in his blood. I, on the other hand, was born in Pennsylvania and grew up in New England. I loved the crisp blue sky of a Vermont fall filled with the vibrant colors of maple leaves and the sparkling white snow of winter.

When I married him, I knew that he wanted eventually to live in Florida. After making several visits to that state, I knew I didn't want to end up there. I thought, why not a compromise in the middle, like Virginia.

Years later our older son unwittingly changed all those ideas when he decided to get married in Monterey, California. A week after attending his wedding in March of 1980, my husband made his announcement.

By the end of the year we had sold our business and our house and headed for California. Since we both grew up in the country, we insisted on having at least an acre of land and were fortunate to find two and a half times that much nestled in among large ranches. It was planted with numerous avocado and citrus trees and a sampling of many other fruits. We had seen avocados in Florida and had even tasted one or two but more than that we didn't know. Nor did we know anything about raising citrus.

We signed up for the avocado school offered through the local extension program. We bought books on western gardening, citrus and exotic fruits. With picker bags on our shoulders, pole picker in one hand, and three-legged ladder in the other, we jumped in with both feet.

Six months later we found ourselves at the local fledgling certified farmers' market learning how to sell our produce. From a modest beginning selling from the tailgate of our little pickup truck half the year, we have expanded to year-round selling with an extensive setup of tables, boxes and baskets.

Our local market itself has grown unbelievably in that time from a handful of growers to well over a hundred in the summer, from a half-year market to a year-round market, and from dying in midmorning to thriving right up to closing time.

This same growth is seen all around the state with more and more markets opening all the time. Chefs come, mayors come, famous people come, and then all of us "ordinary" people come.

Since there are so many unusual products at the farmers' market, either not found in the supermarket at all or found in different forms than at the supermarket, I have found myself answering more and more questions from my customers.

Some years ago Joe Carcione put out a book called *The Greengrocer* which has much useful information if you can find a copy. However, it is geared to the supermarket and has some misleading information for the shopper at the farmers' market, and it doesn't cover many items now found in such markets.

A 1987 publication from *Sunset, Fresh Produce A to Z* is an excellent source of information and I highly recommend it as a companion to this book. It has beautiful color photographs of many varieties of fruits and vegetables. However, it also is geared to commercial markets which import produce when it is out of season here and carry produce not grown in California.

After looking at these books and listening to my customers' questions, it became clear to me that there is a need for a guide specifically geared to the California farmers' markets and farm stands.

Talking to market managers, growers, and customers around the state convinced me that the pamphlet I envisioned needed to be a book. I have done extensive reading. I have attended workshops and gathered information from the Agricultural Commissioner's Office as well as the University of California.

The result of this research is what you hold in your hands. I have tried to arrange the information in a simple manner with a cross-referenced index so that anything may be quickly found, even as you are shopping.

You will find that the amount of information varies widely from one kind of produce to another. In some instances there will be little more than mention of the name, and in other instances there may be several pages of information. The purpose of this book is to provide information that is not already available in other books. For instance, our customers seem to be knowledgeable about turnips and have almost no questions about them so they are mentioned only briefly. However, when strawberry guava are in season, customers have many questions. "What are these?" "Are they ripe?" "How do they grow?" "How do you eat them?" "What do I do with them?" Consequently, there is a great deal more space devoted to them than to turnips.

It is my hope that this book will make shopping at your local farmers' market or farm stand easier and more enjoyable. This is not a coffee table book. It is a working handbook. I have left empty spaces throughout the book for note writing. They should become filled with scribbled notes (the name of your favorite grower for a particular item, some bit of information I neglected to put in the text). The recipe pages should end up with fruit stains and the page corners should become a little dog-eared.

There is a postcard included with this book which I hope you will use to send me suggestions and comments.

Read through the pages of this book to familiarize yourself with the contents. Put it in your shopping basket and head off to your local farmers' market for a grand adventure in shopping, meeting friends, talking to your favorite growers and meeting new ones.

NOTES

CHAPTER 2

DIRECT MARKETING
and
CERTIFIED FARMERS' MARKETS

Direct marketing has proliferated in recent years in the state of California. The term means simply that the consumer buys directly from the grower, eliminating the wholesaler and the commercial retailer.

Roadside Stands
One can buy produce at roadside stands which may be right on a grower's property or may be located in heavy traffic areas. They can carry produce from only one grower (most likely when the stand is right on the grower's property) or may carry produce brought in by growers from various localities (very likely at the stands along well-travelled roads).

U-Pick
Some growers allow customers to do their own picking.

Certified Farmers' Markets
The certified farmers' market is a burgeoning form of direct marketing. All growers selling at such a market must have their property inspected by their county Agricultural Commissioner's Office and display a certificate at their stands. The certificate lists every item of produce which that grower raises and sells at a farmers' market. This procedure guarantees that you are buying directly from the grower, his family or his employee.

Customers are able to look at the certificates at any time to see what the farmer raises and where he does his farming. Ask to see the certificate if it is not prominently displayed. Most customers don't want to bother with such a technicality but it is nice to know that you have this right. Furthermore, the more knowledgeable you become, the more important it will be for you to exercise this right.

Why should you look at the certificate?

Example - to see if a particular kind of produce will be ripe. If you find navel oranges at your market in January, you will want to know where the grower comes from. If he doesn't come from a very southern and warm place, you will be in for a very puckery experience. You certainly would not eat my navel oranges at that time of year. They are still green! And it takes a long time for them to become sweet even after they turn orange.

Another example - to verify that the product on the stand was indeed raised by that grower. Inspectors from the Agricultural Commissioner's Office and market managers are responsible for enforcing market regulations but it is difficult for them to cover all bases.

It is my experience, after helping to manage two markets, that most growers are honest. However, there is the occasional dishonest one and it pays to be a wise and educated shopper. If you come to a certified market you expect fresh produce raised by the owner of the stand. If you suspect that something doesn't "feel right", read the certificate, ask questions, let the manager of the market know of your concerns.

There was a case once of a grower who said he was getting up at 3:00 in the morning to pick for the market. Apparently he *was* getting up then - to go to the Los Angeles wholesale district to "pick" out produce for his stand at the market.

Customers can play an important part in helping to maintain high quality at their market. Managers appreciate customers who care enough about their market to give feedback to them, concerns such as the one just mentioned, or suggestions for improvement. And, of course, compliments are always nice to get.

Until recently, the certificate covered only fruits and vegetables. Such things as honey, eggs and seafood which come under regulation from other branches of government have now been added to the list of products certifiable by the Agricultural Commissioner's Office.

In this book I will be talking about only fruits and vegetables with the one exception of honey.

Unique Characteristics of Farmers' Markets

We have become accustomed to buying almost any kind of produce year round at the supermarket. This has been possible because of imports from other countries (where chemical regulations are much less stringent than in the US, especially California) and because of cold storage and other techniques of this modern age. I'm sure we've all had the misfortune to get a hard unripe tomato that fooled us into thinking it was a vine ripened fruit because of its lovely red color. Gas took care of the color but it remained an unripe fruit.

Produce Is Seasonal

You will need to rethink when you start shopping at a certified farmers' market. An important thing to remember about direct marketing is that only those fruits and vegetables which are in season will be available. It will not be possible to get plums in winter. The supermarket will have them because they import them from South America but they do not grow here in California at that time of year.

Markets will be at their biggest and busiest in the summer months. They will have less variety in the winter. Since many things cannot be grown year round, even a Californian has the chance to freeze and preserve. I always have a certain sense of self-sufficiency and satisfaction when I look at my jars of freshly made jam and

18

pickles or containers ready for the freezer.

Perhaps that comes from my childhood years on our farm in Vermont where we had a large garden for a large family. Most farm families didn't have freezers then so we canned and preserved in huge quantities. I remember layering the carrots in a box of sawdust in the cellar. I also learned what "one rotten apple spoils the barrel" means. That food put away for the long snowy winter gave one a warm sense of security.

Extension of season
Some of the larger growers do use cold storage which can extend the length of their season for certain items. If you want only the very freshest and wish to avoid items which have been in storage, you will want to become familiar with the seasons in your area and those of the growers at your market.

A few growers also have greenhouses to extend the season of limited kinds of produce such as tomatoes.

There is nothing wrong with getting produce that has been in cold storage or grown in a greenhouse as long as you know that is what you are getting and you are aware that it is not going to be the equal in quality of fresh field-grown produce.

Limited Quantities
Because produce is seasonal, there will be shortages, not enough to meet the demand at the beginning and end of the season. Shortages can occur also for other reasons. There may not be enough growers raising a specific item to meet the demand at a particular market. Weather is another important factor in the amount of produce available.

I have become acutely aware of this influence recently with four winters in a row of unusually cold and frosty weather, five years of drought, and a summer with temperatures over 100°. The temperature extremes are unusual for this part of California and I have lost both fruit and flowers.

In the next chapter I will suggest ways of dealing with this situation of shortages.

Produce Is Regional
California is a huge state with widely divergent geography, soils and climates. The *Sunset Western Garden Book* defines 19 climate zones in this state alone. Oranges won't grow in the Sierra Mountains and parsnips won't be any good in San Diego. Therefore, kinds of produce will vary from market to market.

Another regional influence on produce is ethnic. When I visited the Alemany and Heart of the City Markets in San Francisco, I was amazed at all the unusual greens, squash and melons which are used in Asian cooking. Many of the greens are never available at the market where I sell. On the other hand, I saw only one stand with lettuce, whereas at the Santa Barbara markets, you will find lettuce year round in so many varieties that it would take a page or two just to list them in this book.

QUALITY

I would like to be able to tell you that all the produce at farmers' markets is of the very finest quality. Unfortunately, I can't. The reasons vary.

Some growers are very particular about what they put out on their stands, others less so. Some try to pick everything just prior to the market; others pick well ahead. Treatment of the product from harvest to market is very important and varies from one grower to the next. Ripeness at the time of picking is a factor.

The individual grower who does all or most of the work himself, is likely to handle each piece with care. For instance, he can pick one tomato or persimmon at a time, placing it gently into its container, never dumping or pouring. You expect to pay more for this produce.

On the other hand, a large grower with acres of tomato plants or persimmon trees probably does not have the luxury of this kind of handling. You can expect to pay less for the produce that has been piled and poured and picked well ahead, all of which shorten the shelf life of the product.

Some growers wait for maximum maturity before picking, select picking as the days and weeks pass, and bringing only prime fruit. Some growers want to be the first to bring in a particular item so they may start picking before it is quite ready. (Don't we all yearn for the first tomato of the season so badly that we are willing to sacrifice a bit on the ripeness!)

GET TO KNOW THE GROWERS

The more you shop at a farmers' market, the more knowledgeable you will become. Learn what produce is in season in your area. Learn how to judge quality. Also, get to know the growers. You will find that you have favorites who are reliable, who are patient and willing to answer your questions, and who meet your needs.

SPIRIT OF A FARMERS' MARKET

Besides fresh produce, the very nicest thing about shopping at a farmers' market is the atmosphere. I think that being in the outdoors and getting fresh, unwaxed, uncolored, untreated produce to nurture the body, and bouquets of flowers to nurture the soul, is the perfect set of conditions to put us in our best spirits.

The farmers' market is a place to meet friends and to renew ongoing relationships with our favorite farmers, a place to swap recipes, a time to make plans to get together with special friends for the evening.

One day I watched a delightful scene. Two young families bumped into each other and it was clear from their excited words that they hadn't seen each other in some time and that they were joyous at seeing each other again. Then I saw that my grower neighbor, who was watching just as I was, had a big smile on his face. That in turn brought a big smile to my face! Contagious spirit!

Rainy days can be the best of all. There is a certain camaraderie among customers and growers who come out on a rainy day. People who are determined to have their fresh produce and flowers come no matter what the weather. And people who come out in the rain love life. There is an added exuberance on wet days. I have gone home with feet drenched and co-o-old, only to find myself in the highest of spirits.

I hope all my readers will brave a rainy day market just once, preferably done up in waterproof gear.

MARKET FLAVOR

In doing the research for this book, I have had the pleasure of visiting a number of markets in different cities and towns. Each one has its own flavor and I would encourage you to visit markets other than your own any time you are traveling around our state.

There are big ones and there are little ones. Some have baked and canned goods for sale as well as produce. Some have musicians performing live music, which can be anything from a solo recorder to a complete steel band. Special events like "back to the farm" days in the fall or madrigal singers at Christmas add to the lure of farmers' markets. Each market is a new adventure.

For information on direct marketing in your area:
Call your local Agricultural Commissioner's office listed in the white government pages of your phone book.

For statewide information, write to:
Small Farm Center
University of California
Davis, CA 95616-8699
Tel. (916) 757 8579

This center puts out a statewide directory of farmers' market locations and hours, roadside stands and U-pick operations.

NOTES

CHAPTER 3

SHOPPING AT THE MARKET

BASKETS AND BAGS

Some of my customers have become expert at juggling bags while picking out produce and getting the correct change out of a hand full of coins with only that hand to work with. I admire their expertise as I think of my own clumsy style (which I chalk off to my lack of experience on that side of the stand).

The customers who have their shopping technique most refined are the ones who have been buying from me for many years. They have one thing that other shoppers don't have, a large rather shallow **basket** with a high handle. The large base allows for the separation of more fragile things which a smaller deeper basket doesn't allow. The basket can be put on the ground while one is selecting produce without letting things spill as is apt to happen with plastic bags. Bunches of long-stemmed flowers rest safely on top so the shopper's hands are both free.

Large **canvas tote bags** seem to work very well because they are sturdy and easy to carry, can be put on the ground without spilling and hold a lot. The shortcoming is the difficulty in carrying fragile things such as berries and ripe peaches. There are several solutions to this problem with **tote bags and deeper baskets**. You can buy sturdy produce first so it starts out on the bottom or, more realistically, rearrange as necessary so sturdy ends up on the bottom and fragile on the top.

Rearranging can be time consuming and cumbersome, however, so an ideal solution is simply to take along **covered plastic containers** of sizes appropriate for your planned purchases. Then you can buy blackberries first thing before they are sold out and tuck them safely in the bottom of your basket or bag.

Other containers are **string bags**, those European shopping bags that look so small but can expand and expand, **cartons**, **shopping carts** (check the wheels because they seem to have a tendency to fall off), and **wagons** (no need to have a child as an excuse to pull one of these).

In addition, bring some of the **paper and plastic bags** you have acquired through other shopping. Together at a farmers' market we can make a major impact on the environment. If there are 100 growers at a market and the average number of purchases from each grower is 100, that equals 10,000 bags, just in the period of a few hours. Multiply that figure times all the markets throughout the state times 52 weeks in the year and the numbers are impressive. With a little planning ahead and some effort at developing new habits, we actually could eliminate most of those bags.

I do try to encourage my customers to add new purchases to bags they already have, thus maximizing the use of each bag. I also encourage them to omit a bag completely if they have a basket, tote bag, or other such container and their purchase can be placed in it loosely.

Suggestion: Save all those berry baskets, berry carrier boxes, net bags and other special packaging and return them to the grower they came from or any other grower who can use them. We growers appreciate these donations.

RATTLED?

Some of our markets are quite new and still pleasantly small so shopping at them is a delight. For those of you who shop at the bigger markets there can be problems which we will look at here.

Parking: If you have difficulty parking your first time or two, don't get discouraged. Experience will tell you where to park, and the managers or assistants can be very helpful to you in this matter. Don't hesitate to ask for their help.

If the parking seems too far away when you are returning to your car laden with baskets and bags of produce and flowers, see if your market offers a shuttle between the market site and the parking lots. If they don't and you think there is enough need to justify it, you might sound out the management on starting such a shuttle service.

Crowds: If crowds overwhelm you, ask the manager when the quietest time at the market is and plan to shop at that time. It may be that the quietest time will be later in the market when commodities in short supply are gone. You lose the opportunity to buy those items but you gain peace of mind, a tradeoff that may well be worthwhile to you.

Short supply/Big demand: This problem comes about from three causes. One is the nature of direct marketing which limits produce to that which is in season. The second is simply that there may not be enough growers coming to the local market with a particular product or the growers coming with that product aren't large enough to meet the need. The third reason may be that a particular grower has produce of exceptional quality which most likely equates with limited quantity.

This situation can lead to lines, or even less desirable than lines, a crowd with no order. The result can be frustration and disappointment for the shopper.

Here are some suggestions for coping positively with the problem.

1. Give up. No,no. Just joking. Besides, that's not positive!

2. If a crowd arrangement leaves you always at the back because others are more aggressive and you always miss out on the product, wait until the crush is over and recommend to the grower that he set up a roped line system such as those commonly used in banks now.

3. Arrive early at the market and check with the grower to see what time his crowd or line starts forming. You can then have the advantage of being at the beginning of the line.

4. Get an idea of how much of the product the grower was able to bring. Is it all out on display or is there more to be put out? This will help you decide if it is worth your while to stand in line.

5. Ask the grower if he plans to limit the quantity a customer may buy.

After sizing up these factors, you can make a deliberate decision about whether to stand in line or not.

If you opt for the line, it can prove to be one of the best parts of your shopping trip. A grower whose stand is next to mine is pretty much a one-person operation. Her trademark is exceptional quality. There is just so much one person can raise which means a limited quantity. This means she always has a very long line. It has to go somewhere and it goes in front of my stand.

She was quite concerned that it might have a negative impact on me. I reassured her that I had no objections. Listening to the local classical music radio station, which I leave turned on in my van, has become a part of the early morning setup. If I forget to turn it on, there is always a customer to remind me. This leads, inevitably, to several of us trying to figure out what is playing and even to discussions about where to buy compact discs.

We discuss yellow limes and the environment. My neighbor's customers have even helped me set up when they could see that I had more than I could handle by myself.

I also offer a "place your order at this end of my stand and pick it up at the other end" service which allows them to buy from me without losing their place in my neighbor's line.

Moral: lines can be fun!

However, if I haven't convinced you to stand in line, you might want to look into placing an order with the grower. Not all growers will do this because the customer forgets to come by the next week to get his order and the grower is left with lettuce that will wilt or berries that will mold and no money for them.

To place orders:

> Offer to pay for your order when you place it.
>
> Or, arrange with the grower to put your order out on his stand if you haven't picked it up by a specified time.
>
> Exchange telephone numbers in case either of you runs into unexpected circumstances during the week intervening.
>
> These arrangements protect the grower, who, after all, is there to sell his goods. It also takes pressure off you if you should get tied up unexpectedly.

TOO MUCH TO CARRY?

There are growers who will be happy to let you store your purchases at their stands as you accumulate them, perhaps inside their vehicle or right next to it.

Some markets provide services for helping the customer with overburdened arms. Check with the manager of your market to see if any such service is offered. If not, ask if they would consider providing one.

CAUTION - PROTECT YOUR MONEY

Keep your billfold or purse on your person or well hidden. A coin purse sitting in the top of a basket is, regrettably, a prime target for theft.

NOTES FROM MARKET MANAGERS

There are a number of things customers can do to help make their market run smoothly.

1. Respect **markers for traffic flow** such as orange traffic cones and sawhorses. They are meant for *all* people and are very important for the safety of everyone present.

2. Respect the **starting time for selling**. It is a tremendous help to the growers to have time to set up before selling begins. It is very difficult to try to set up and sell at the same time. Think of growers' stands as stores which don't open their doors until the official opening time.

3. The extension of #2 is not to pick out or bag produce before opening time. That is the same thing as buying except that the money hasn't changed hands.

4. Have respect for all **signs** such as "no parking", "please refrain from smoking", "no animals allowed" or "no pets allowed". Regarding the latter, in particular **dogs**, I want to elaborate.

When we think of a farm, we think of a dog running free over the acres, and probably most of the growers are dog lovers who have their own dog. But the health department does not allow any pets at a market. Yes, we understand that your dog is perfectly behaved and the best one around.

But, the health department does not believe you and can actually shut the market down if the inspector comes while your dog is in the market. The reason behind this ruling is that dogs drop hairs which can end up in the food. Worse, they have been seen to lift a leg and urinate on the produce for sale.

There is always the concern in a public place that a dog might bite someone.

Please leave your dog outside the market grounds.

5. Please walk **bicycles**. It can be very dangerous to ride a bicycle through a market with so many people moving about. You never know when a child might run unexpectedly into your path or a customer back up into you.

CHAPTER 4

GROWERS' PET PEEVES

The Uninvited Sampler: Style I

This is the person who helps himself to a berry (usually the biggest, of course) from a basket or pulls grapes from a bunch, or otherwise creates a gap in the produce.

If you sample produce from a container or bunch, the purchaser of that container or bunch will be short changed. Surely, you wouldn't want to buy it.

If you want a taste, ask the grower.

Maybe it is the Yankee in me, but I resent people who simply help themselves to my wares (unless, of course, I have a basket labeled "samples"). But if a customer is kind enough to ask, I enjoy doing my best to provide a sample.

The Uninvited Sampler: Style II

This is the person who snaps beans in half and discards the pieces in the box while picking out whole beans to purchase.

He shells the beans.

He rips ears of corn open.

He opens a peapod, eats the peas and throws the shell back into the display of peas.

Again, please ask the grower for a sample, please respect his produce, and hang onto the shells or hulls or pits until you find an appropriate place to put them. No, no! Not on the ground or under the display table. They won't decompose there to go back into the ground and the poor grower who's pooped by the end of the market has to clean up all your garbage.

The Disregarder Of Signs

This is the customer who sees the signs posted by the growers, reads them and then proceeds to disregard them. He may even go so far as to improvise a justification for his disregard.

When a particular fruit or vegetable is in very short supply, e.g. tomatoes in December, the grower may post a sign asking customers to limit their purchase to a certain number of pieces in order to share the "wealth". If you are tenth in line, you will appreciate the customers in front of you respecting that limit so there will be some for you. By the same token, the customers behind you will appreciate your respecting the limit so there will be some for them.

The Greedy One

This customer comes in various styles. He may be the one who purchases a basket of berries, pays for them and then proceeds to remove berries from other baskets to fill his own to overflowing.

He may be the one who sneaks an extra piece or two into the bag and doesn't pay for it.

He may be one who has a bit of trouble being that dishonest so he counts out the number he says he is going to buy and then picks up another piece and looks at the grower with a hopeful expression on his face or even pleads with begging eyes to have that one for free.

He may be the kind who makes a big to-do about getting out his money to pay the grower and while he is busy making this big to-do, he slowly eases out of the picture and melts into the market without giving the grower so much as a penny.

And then there is the customer who comes to the stand and sees the beautifully tree ripened lemons at 20c each. The grocery store is selling month-old under-ripe waxed lemons for twice that much *and* he asks the grower if he will sell them to him for 10c each.

Please remember that farming does not a rich man make.

The Pincher
This is the customer who picks up the avocado or persimmon or peach with thumb and forefinger, very carefully making a point of keeping all other fingers well out of the way, and then proceeds to test for ripeness by forcing the thumb and forefinger toward each other. Now when I have a customer do this with a newly picked rock hard avocado, I hold up quite well. But when he does this to the piece of fruit that has ripened to perfection without any bruises, I have a moment of panic and gain another gray hair!

Please don't pinch the fruit. You don't really want all the growers to turn white-haired before their time, do you? The correct way to test such fruits for ripeness is to hold the piece in the palm of your hand and gently feel the whole.

The Ash Dropper
This customer is the cigarette smoker who in all likelihood is disregarding "Please refrain from smoking" signs posted around the market site. As the cigarette dangling from his lips burns away, the ash grows longer and longer and as he leans over the magnificent head of leaf lettuce, the grower behind the stand is going into a panic as the ash threatens to fall all over the damp fresh green leaves.

Please delay your cigarette until after you are done shopping.

The Ripper
This is the person who rips leaves off the lettuce or pulls them from the center of the head and then leaves the damaged head behind. The grower will have to reduce the price for some other customer or take the damaged product back to his farm for composting.

Lettuce growers always have stray outer leaves which they will be happy to share with you if you want to taste different varieties.

Impressive Bills of the $50 and $100 Denominations
Please be kind enough to leave these bills at home and bring the smaller varieties.

The Pusher and Shover
This is the customer who was there "first" no matter what time he joined the group at a particular stand.

A grower who is trying to wait on ten people at once welcomes patience and kind words from the waiting customers. Especially welcome are the words "He was here first. I don't mind waiting."

NOTES

CHAPTER 5

ORGANIC - WHAT IS IT?

One grower was selling at an evening market when a reporter for one of the local newspapers approached and, looking at the dahlias, asked "Are they organic?"

"Well, I guess so but I wouldn't recommend that you eat them."

With that, the poor reporter realized what a misplaced question she had asked. But it points up the great concern for organic produce these days, even though many cannot agree on quite what the term means.

Underlying the concern, of course, is the desire on the part of all of us to ingest as little in the way of harmful substances as possible and to cause a minimum of negative impact on our environment.

Important Note

There is a misconception among many customers that "farmers' market" equates with "organic". Direct marketing regulations do not have any requirements regarding growing methods, which means that produce has been raised in many different ways. It would be possible for an individual farmers' market to set a local policy of having only organic farmers but that policy would be limited to that market. With few exceptions farmers' markets have a mix of organic and conventional growers.

ORGANIC AGRICULTURE

Organic, in the very simplest of terms means using only the following in the raising of crops: animal and plant material, both living and decaying, naturally-occurring minerals, and physical action such as old-fashioned weeding. This means that no synthetic materials are used.

There are, however, modern day exceptions to this. Organic farmers do use certain manufactured materials such as Safer Soap. It is also important to remember that "organic" does not mean chemical-free.

State regulations: The state of California has a set of strict regulations which a grower must meet in order to call himself organic and he must have met them for a period of one to three years minimum before he can lay claim to being organic.

Any grower who uses the terms **organic, organically grown, naturally grown, ecologically grown, biologically grown,** or **wild,** must meet the requirements of California Assembly Bill 2012 known as the Organic Food Act of 1990.

CCOF - California Certified Organic Farmers: You will see some farmers with signs stating that they are members of the CCOF. This is a self-regulating group which sets somewhat more restrictive standards and you are assured that they meet all the current requirements for organic farming.

However, not all organic farmers choose to belong to this organization so there will be growers at your market who meet organic requirements even though they do not post this formal sign. In fact, only about 20% of all organic farmers belong to this organization so if you buy only "organic" produce, do not limit yourself to buying just from growers displaying this symbol.

There are several other organizations of organic growers which will undoubtedly grow in the next few years.

Beginning in 1994, the law requires that all growers claiming to be organic must be certified by a third party organization such as CCOF or one of the lesser known organic groups.

CONVENTIONAL AGRICULTURE

Most growers fit into this category and variation from grower to grower is great. Some growers use synthetic fertilizers, insecticides, fungicides, herbicides, and growth regulators. Other growers may use only one or two of these synthetic materials and rely on organic methods for other aspects of their farming. They may grow some of their crops conventionally and some organically. They may have a portion of their operation certified organic but the rest not.

Just what a particular farmer does depends on his philosophy, his crops, his environmental conditions, the size of his operation and market demands, crop insurance company requirements, and lenders' requirements.

State regulations: Just as the state regulates organic farming, it regulates conventional farming, and restrictions are becoming ever tighter. California has the most restrictive regulations of all of our fifty states.

Farm supply distributors must keep detailed records of all sales of pesticides (product, quantity, purchaser, and other pertinent information). And they must have on file each grower's operator identification number for use of non-restricted pesticides as well as grower permits for the use of restricted pesticides. They must file regular reports with the County Agricultural Commissioner's Office.

The grower who buys from a farm supply distributor must have an Operator Identification number in order to buy *any* pesticide. For certain pesticides he must have a special permit and meet even more stringent requirements, such as soil testing to prove the need for the material. Without such proof of need, he is not permitted to buy the material. The grower must file monthly reports with the County Agricultural Commissioner's Office stating what products he used that month, in what quantity, over what acreage, and other required information.

At the time of this writing, any home gardener can go into any neighborhood home and garden center and get many pesticides with no restrictions whatsoever.

Although he is required to follow the label directions, it is almost impossible for our government agencies to enforce his safe and responsible use of the product. This means that an irresponsible person can go home, apply the materials any way he pleases and then go off to the beach for the rest of the day without being accountable for his application. I mention this to emphasize the responsibility that is used in the regulated farming industry.

If you want to keep your life extremely simple, you may want to stop reading at this point and move on to the next chapter. But please don't do that. This issue of "organic" is so complex and so important to all of us that I hope you will read on and become informed enough to make decisions that are well suited to both your physical and emotional needs.

Did you know

that organic growers use sprays?

that conventional growers do not necessarily use sprays?

that cryocite (manufactured) is the same as cryolite (naturally occurring)?

that steer manure (organic) can contain antibiotics and hormones as well as fly spray?

that fish emulsion (organic) can contain mercury?

that nitrogen from organic plant material can seep into the ground water just as readily as nitrogen from manufactured fertilizer?

that carcinogens occur naturally in produce?

These are but a handful of questions we need to think about if we are to become well-informed and responsible consumers. Unfortunately, organic versus conventional agriculture is not a simple good versus bad, black and white issue. It is a complex set of grays.

Here are some things to keep in mind as you shop.

Pesticide Residues

The World Health Organization and/or the U.S. Environmental Protection Agency set the standards for the amount of synthetic pesticide residue which is allowed on fruits and vegetables at harvest. The amount varies according to the material and produce involved and has a multiplication factor for a buffer. Look in Section V of this book to learn where you can get detailed information on this subject.

According to federal standards, organic produce can legally have synthetic pesticide residue if it is less than 10% of the federal tolerance for that crop.

In reality, most produce, even that which is raised conventionally, has no detectable residue at the time you purchase it. And in most cases where there is residue, the amount meets the standards set for organic produce. Human exposure to pesticides by way of food is extremely low. Again, for greater details on this subject, turn to Section V for sources.

Food Safety, Spring 1989, Vol. 2 Issue 2 discusses a paper released in April 1989 by the Institute for Food Technologists with the consensus of 14 professional societies representing 100,000 toxicologists, microbiologists, and food technologists. "The paper specifically notes that `the primary hazard present in the American food supply is posed by pathogenic organisms (i.e., bacteria and their toxins and viruses), not by pesticides.' "

Unofficial Terms
Because of the wide variation in farming methods, several terms have come into use, such as "unsprayed" and "no pesticides". These are unofficial terms so you, the consumer, need to become knowledgeable enough to ask specific questions.

Unsprayed: When the grower says he uses no sprays, is he talking about insecticides only or does he mean that he uses no sprays including fungicides, herbicides, growth regulators and minerals?

No pesticides: When he says he uses no pesticides, does he mean only that he does not spray pesticides on the plant itself or does he mean that he uses no pesticides in the soil as well? Does he mean that he uses no synthetic pesticides but does use organically approved pesticides such as mined sulphur, bordeaux mixes, or antibiotics such as streptomycin?

Disagreement and Confusion
The current State of California laws governing organic farming are undergoing reevaluation and there is disagreement even among organic growers as to how the law should read.

To illustrate the complexities involved, let's look at Thompson seedless grape horticulture as it exists under current interpretations of organic and conventional farming. The grapes can be allowed to grow untouched from bud to mature grape. The bunches will be fairly tight and the grapes small, about 1/2 inch long. They will most likely have mildew since grapes are very susceptible to this pest. These are organic grapes assuming soil amendments were organic.

To increase the size of the grapes, a growth regulator or hormone may be used. It needs to be used several times throughout the growing period, the first application being at the start of the bloom to cause flowers to fall off, reducing the number of grapes in the bunch. After all, if they are going to be bigger grapes, room needs to be made for them so they don't press against each other and crack open, leading to rotting and insect problems. There needs to be room also for air between the grapes to discourage mildew.

The growth regulator is sprayed again at intervals to encourage the fruit to become large, close to an inch in length or more. Those in the supermarket are all raised this way.

The growth hormone which is known as gibberellic acid occurs naturally in the grapes. The grower is simply adding more to what is already there. However, what he adds is not naturally occurring. It is manufactured. Based upon the definition of organic which I gave you, that means that grapes raised with the addition of gibberellic acid are not organic.

Not necessarily true! Gibberellic acid is manufactured by two companies. That which comes from one company is allowed in organic farming. That which comes from the other is not.

To prevent mildew on grapes, which is a serious problem, sulphur spray can be used. If the sulphur is mined, it is considered organic. If the sulphur is a natural by-product of gas refining, it is not considered organic.

Because of the varying interpretations of what is organic as shown in this example, I would suggest that instead of asking a grower if he is organic, that you ask how he farms. One grower I know, when asked "Are you organic?" chooses to take the "you" literally. She holds out one arm, then the other, looks at them, then looks up and down her body and replies "Yes, I believe I am." She recognizes the complexity of the issue and likes to discuss farming methods.

Choices

In some cases you may have to choose between organic produce which has mildew or fungus (naturally occurring toxins and carcinogens in fungi are being studied and are believed to be a health risk) and conventionally grown produce treated with a fungicide that leaves no residue and has no mildew or fungus. It is a trade off and the better you understand the farming process, the easier it will be to make a decision that is right for you.

I had an interesting experience that I share with customers. I have discovered that the best control of scale insect on my lemons is to leave the situation to nature. When we first bought our place the lemons looked beautiful. As the years passed they developed scale which became so severe that I stood at my sink every Friday night in preparation for the Saturday morning market scrubbing the miserable little creatures off to meet the agricultural standards. I told myself that we had to do something about this time-consuming situation. The least toxic solution was an agricultural oil spray, but it had to be applied when the weather wasn't too hot and when the weather wasn't too cold, and I just never got around to it when the conditions were right.

However, the little creatures began to subside and we have settled into a nice situation where the scale and their natural predators live in balance. We always have a little scale but I don't spend Friday night at my sink scrubbing and I don't spray.

In this case, customers can make a choice between my lemons with no pesticides of any kind but with a few scale or someone else's lemons with no scale but which have been treated with pesticide at some point and in all likelihood do not have any detectable residue.

Balance and the Big Picture

We need to remember that the farmer who does nothing but plant, water, and physically weed his garden is an organic farmer. But, because he is not adding any soil amendments, he is depleting his precious soil. There is an important balance between what we put into our farming and what we take out.

I attended a workshop given by Richard Alan Miller who specializes in herbs. He says he doesn't like the term "organic". He prefers to talk about "regenerative agriculture". I like that terminology because it seems to remove the emotion from the subject, to require balance, and to keep what I call the "big picture" in mind. This overall balance is far more important than words like "organic".

Here is a "bigger picture" to ponder. There are insects and other little creatures which feast on strawberries. A grower can use synthetic pesticides to control the pests and meet all regulations regarding residue, bringing safe healthy berries to market. Or, because of the demand for "organic" produce, the grower can control these pests by vacuuming them up each morning. These berries come to market as safe healthy berries.

If these berries were side by side at the market, we would choose the vacuumed berries. After all, why bother taking the chance of even a minuscule pesticide residue when we don't have to?

Enter the bigger picture. The vacuum cleaner requires fossil fuel for operation. We have a finite amount of fossil fuel. Furthermore, the vacuum cleaner's exhaust puts contaminants into the air. Not to mention the fossil fuel needed to manufacture the vacuuming equipment and the contaminants that process puts in the air.

So the question might be "Which form of farming is less detrimental to the environment as a whole and to ourselves?"

Perhaps the answer doesn't lie in choosing one or the other but rather in doing away with both forms of insect control. Perhaps we, as consumers, need to reevaluate our demand for perfect appearance in our produce.

Our world is extremely complex and actions halfway around the world affect us without our even realizing it. The burning of the Amazon rain forest is a dramatic example.

On the local level, we need to be realistic about this word "organic". The steer manure that the organic farmer puts in his soil may itself contain trace amounts of antibiotics and growth hormones which are routinely fed to beef cattle. The fish emulsion may be tainted with mercury.

An unsprayed orchard may fall victim to overspray from a helicopter traversing the neighbor's hundreds of acres.

My philosophy on this matter is to avoid, whenever I can, substances which are potentially harmful, but not to worry about factors that are beyond my control. I believe the worry is more harmful to our bodies than any substance allowed in California farming.

Read any articles you come across in newspapers and magazines about conventional farming and organic farming to broaden your understanding and keep abreast of new findings.

So go ahead and ask if the fruit or vegetables are organic (or better yet, ask how the grower does his farming). But don't forget to bring the "bigger picture" along with you when you pack up to go to the market.

NOTES

CHAPTER 6

DEFINITIONS

Following are a few definitions as they pertain to this book.

Fruits and Vegetables

I most often use these words with their common meanings rather than with their botanic meanings. Most of what we refer to as fruits are botanically fruits although there are a few exceptions such as rhubarb which is actually a vegetable used as a fruit.

Any vegetable which has seeds is botanically a fruit but if we use it as a vegetable I include it in the vegetable section of this book. Tomatoes, beans, okra, and corn, for instance, are actually fruit but we commonly call them vegetables and I include them in the vegetable section.

Ripe and Mature

These words can lead to some confusion so for the purposes of this book, we will be using the following definitions.

Ripe means mature and ready to eat.

Maturity refers to an amount of growth which takes place while the fruit or vegetable is still on the plant. It is important to us mostly in regard to fruit in its botanical meaning. That is, as it pertains to corn and beans as well as plums and peaches. We judge maturity by such things as sugar content (pears), color (red peppers) and oil content (avocados).

In the case of such things as snap beans and cucumbers, we actually harvest well before maturity is reached because these fruits do not need to be "ripe" before we eat them.

In some fruits, full maturity and ripeness are achieved simultaneously such as strawberry guava and blackberries. These fruits are ready to eat at the time of harvest and they are not harvested until they are ready to eat.

In other fruits, such as feijoa and avocados, maturity precedes ripeness . These fruits must stand in your kitchen to become soft and "ripe" after harvest.

There are still other fruits, such as peaches and plums, which can be picked either way. That is, they can be picked mature but not quite ripe and ready to eat or they can be picked at the point when they are simultaneously mature and ripe.

In these last two groups mentioned, maturity can have a range from minimum to maximum, the range being very wide for avocados and very narrow for peaches. In these two groups, minimum maturity must be attained for the fruit to ripen properly after picking and maximum maturity equates with finest quality.

Notes Regarding Recipes

In all cases where recipes were contributed by other people, I have given the creator of each recipe credit either in the title of the recipe or at the end of the recipe.

All other recipes, those without a contributor's name, are creations of my own.

Abbreviations used in recipes are as follows:

    c = cup

    t = teaspoon

    T = tablespoon

When canning and preserving, always follow the latest directions from the manufacturers of canning jars. See Section V for sources of information.

FRUITS

APPLES

An apple orchard had been planted on our Vermont farm long before our family called it home. There were giant Wolf River apples and small Strawberry apples, McIntosh, yellow transparent, Baldwin and many other kinds whose names I don't remember after all these years.

I loved to climb into an old Wolf River tree which had a perfect branch for relaxing in the shade on a hot summer day. One McIntosh tree I remember in particular was along the road where we passed every school day on the half mile walk to the school bus. I felt a certain excitement when those apples became ripe because they were a treat on the way to or from school.

My mother made apple jelly, mint jelly (an apple based jelly), apple sauce, apple pie and apple crisps from those delicious old varieties. We stored barrels of apples in our basement for the long winter months.

Many of those old-fashioned varieties are gone or very rare. Happily there are growers who are tracking down and raising many of them. I think we will again be able to enjoy some of those unusual varieties, thanks to the popularity of farmers' markets nationwide.

Pearl and Ed Munak of Paso Robles have planted some of these old varieties. Like so many of our growers, they have a very interesting background. They were living in Los Angeles where Ed was a systems engineer and Pearl earned a law degree. One day they decided to move out of that smoggy congested city to the nice rural town of Paso Robles where they bought a farm in 1977.

They have been organic growers since 1985, farming 154 acres with melons, apples, tomatoes, peppers, and cattle. They market their produce through farmers' markets, organic wholesale and gourmet wholesale.

"We do not grow any ordinary fruit," says Pearl. They choose unusual varieties of each of the kinds of produce they grow, specializing in outstanding flavor. The climate in Paso Robles is ideal for producing sweetness in fruit, with hot clear days and cool nights. Pearl tells me that "apples from our area were proven sweetest in the state by tests at UC Davis". In their orchard she and Ed are trying to bring back some of the older apple varieties.

Varieties
Here are some of the varieties found at our markets:

Gala - one of the earliest varieties to appear. An excellent eating apple, sweet and crisp, it is red and yellow in color and may resemble a nectarine with red blush over the yellow background color. This apple has an interesting background. Cox's Orange Pippin, a favorite in England, and Red Delicious are crossed to make Kidd's

Orange Red. This Kidd's Orange Red is then crossed with Golden Delicious to make the Gala.

Gordon - a red and gold apple which can be very large. It has a low chill factor so can be grown along the coast where the climate remains mild through the winter. Picked before maturity, the background color will be green and the flavor tart and excellent. Picked at maturity, the background will be golden yellow and the apple will be quite sweet.

Granny Smith - a large light to yellow green tart apple, fine textured and excellent for storing and cooking. Slices hold their shape nicely in pies.

Gravenstein - red and gold striped, tart, good for eating fresh and excellent for applesauce because it breaks down when cooked.

McIntosh - a red apple, tangy and firm, excellent for eating.

Mutsu - called Crispin in England. Another Golden Delicious cross but larger and firmer than the Delicious and slightly more tart. Good cooking and storage.

Pippin - a yellow green to yellow apple with russeting around stem end. Another tart apple which holds its shape nicely in pies.

Rome Beauty - a red apple which is semi-tart and excellent for baking as it holds its shape well.

Selecting
Color is the most important quality to look for in judging the maturity of an apple. In apples which are "striped" like the Gravenstein, look at the background color, not the red. The background should be creamy or yellow. If it is green, the apple was picked before reaching maturity. It will be more tart than the apples picked at maturity.

Solid green apples should actually be pale green or yellowish. The Granny Smith which is very common in our markets is almost always sold very green. Opt for yellower ones if you have the chance as they are more mature and therefore sweeter.

Yellow apples picked green will lighten and become more yellow as they stand.

In solid red apples, choose the richest colored fruit. The color will not change after picking.

In all cases, the better the color, which indicates maturity, the sweeter and more flavorful the apple will be.

Firmness is another trait to look for. The longer apples have been off the tree, the softer they get and the shorter their shelf life once you get them.

Shape and size are not factors in selecting apples.

Sunburn, which appears as a brownish spot on one side, affects the keeping quality of the fruit. It is not a problem if you plan to use the apples soon. You may be able to get a good buy on a quantity of these for making applesauce where you peel the apples anyway and appearance is irrelevant.

Sugar content (sweetness) is affected not only by maturity, but by the climate as well. This means that any particular variety can vary from year to year and grower to grower.

Using

We think of apples as eating apples or cooking apples. In reality, you can do both with any apple, but some varieties are better for eating fresh and others are ideal for cooking.

For eating fresh choose softer, sweeter varieties. For cooking choose firmer, tarter varieties. They hold up much better in cooking and can be sweetened during the cooking.

Softer varieties have a coarser texture and aren't always good keepers. An excellent example is the Golden Delicious which is truly delicious when freshly picked and still firm. As it sits, it becomes softer and almost mealy.

Fine-textured varieties tend to be firmer and are usually good keepers and cookers.

Generally speaking, the earlier varieties tend to be coarser textured and later varieties tend to be finer textured.

Season

Apples first start coming into the markets in late July and can be found through fall and winter and into the spring if the grower has a large enough crop and good storage.

RECIPES

Apple and Sauerkraut Bake

Shredded apple	2 T orange juice concentrate
Rinsed, squeezed sauerkraut	2 T Bavarian mustard (contains seeds)
Mace	

Place equal parts apple and sauerkraut in shallow casserole. Sprinkle with mace. Mix orange juice and mustard together and pour over apple mixture. Bake 45 minutes at 350°.

Hebe says this dish is especially good with boiled bratwurst.

Hebe Bartz

Judith Reynolds' Apple Dessert

Apples
Raisins
Cinnamon

Peel, core and slice desired amount of apples into a microwave-safe dish. Add generous amount of raisins and sprinkle cinnamon over top. Stir gently to mix slightly. Place in microwave. Cook on high power approximately 5 minutes, stir gently, then finish cooking on high until apples are soft.

The actual cooking time will vary depending upon the quantity being prepared, the firmness of the apples, and the power of the microwave.

Serve hot or cold. If you want to dress this dessert up a bit, try topping with one of the following:

    unsweetened whipped cream flavored with vanilla

    nonfat plain or vanilla yogurt

    frozen yogurt

Apple Oat Dessert

Sliced apples   1/4 c margarine
1 t cinnamon   1/4 c oat bran
Raisins   1/4 c wheat bran
     3/4 c quick oats

Prepare and slice enough apples to fill 12" quiche pan. Sprinkle with cinnamon and as many raisins as desired.

Mix oat and wheat bran together, cut in margarine, add quick oats and stir. Spread this topping over apples.

Bake at 375° 25-30 minutes.

AVOCADOS

California is famous for avocados, and the shopper at the farmers' market has the chance to try far more varieties than anyone who does all his shopping at the grocery store.

Varieties and Seasons

One can get avocados year round at the market, and the season for any particular variety is longer at the market than at the grocery store. This is because the grower can pick the fruit as early as the commercial grower but can pick much later than the commercial grower since he can bring the fruit directly to market without the long delays of packing houses and cold storage. Also, he can bring the last of the season's fully mature fruit which is too fragile or short-lived to make it to the supermarket.

The most familiar variety is Hass, which is the bumpy-skinned fruit that turns very dark when it is ripe. There are a few other varieties which become dark but most varieties remain green when they are ready to eat.

It is easy to list variety names but defining their seasons is difficult because the climate in which the trees are grown is a significant factor. We will start by looking at the statewide picture and then I will explain how to choose the best avocados in your area.

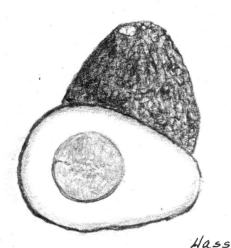

Hass

Some of the varieties found at our markets and their statewide availability are:

Hass: all year

Fuerte: winter

Bacon: late winter through late spring

Rincon: spring into summer

MacArthur: late fall into winter

Selecting

In order to determine the best to buy at any given time in your particular area, there are two factors to consider: climate and oil content.

Climate

Keep in mind that any given variety grown in a warmer climate such as San Diego or Ojai will mature earlier than that same variety grown along the cooler coastal regions like Santa Barbara.

If you are buying a variety at the very beginning of its season, it should come from a warmer climate. If you are buying at the very end of the season, it will come only from the cooler region as the warm area fruit will be gone. During the main part of the season, it will be available from both areas.

Oil Content

Fruit maturity is judged by oil content.

At maximum maturity Hass has the highest oil content of all avocados and Bacon probably has about the lowest oil content of the varieties you will find at the market. Other varieties range in between.

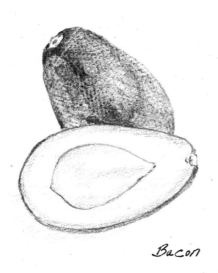

Bacon

In all avocados, the longer the fruit remains on the tree, the higher the oil content will become. The Rincon has the reputation of being a very poor watery fruit. When we belonged to a co-op and harvested the Rincon when they prescribed, it truly was inferior. After we left the co-op and started marketing our own fruit, we left the Rincons on the tree until they started dropping. Behold, they turned out to be a superb fruit with excellent oil content and flavor.

The later it is in the season for any particular variety, the better that fruit will be.

The key, then, is to get the fruit which has been on the tree longest. If, in January or February, you have the choice of getting new crop Hass or end of the season MacArthur, get the latter because it will have the better flavor and oil content. This applies to any of the varieties.

Identifying immature fruit

An avocado that has not been on the tree long enough will not ripen properly. It will instead become very rubbery and be rather "green" in flavor. It will appear too shiny and the green will be too bright. Most avocados will start to lose their shiny appearance as they become high enough in oil content for good quality. The one exception to this that I am aware of is in the Hass. Sometimes at the end of its season, the smoother skinned fruit of this variety will be very shiny when dark but will be superb in quality.

Size
Varieties range from the small Anna through medium Hass to huge Pinkerton. Within any variety the size will vary greatly but has little bearing on the quality of the fruit. If you want a small serving, get a small fruit. If you want to stuff the avocado, get a large fruit. The seed will be proportionately larger or smaller so you need not fear that the small fruit will be all seed and a poor buy.

Hard or soft - which to get
Avocados never soften on the tree. They soften only after they have been picked or have dropped onto the ground. Avocados that drop are perfectly good and are often the very best because they don't drop until they are fully mature. There is an important exception to this statement. Fruit that drops early in the season before it has developed an adequate oil content will not be any good and it is part of nature's pruning process. It is the drop late in the season that is so fine.

When choosing your fruit keep the foregoing information in mind. Now that you have determined which variety is at its mature best, you need to decide whether you want ripe or unripe fruit. There is always an abundance of hard fruit so with a little planning ahead, your shopping will be easier if you get the hard fruit each week and let it ripen in your kitchen. If you must have ripe fruit for that day or within the next day or two, arrive at the market early and get in line if need be so you won't be disappointed.

Testing fruit for ripeness:
Hold the whole fruit in the palm of your hand to get the feel of the total. Only very slight even pressure is needed to tell if the fruit is ready. **Please don't pinch** it because that won't alert you to dubious spots and in fact will damage the fruit if it is already soft. Do not press on the stem end to test for ripeness as this will merely cause damage if the fruit is ready to eat.

The fruit should be evenly soft all over. A bruised spot can be removed just as in an apple or peach but beware of a soft spot on an otherwise hard fruit.

Do not judge quality by the presence or absence of the stem. Hard fruit properly picked will have the stem on. Fruit that has dropped off the tree at maturity will not have a stem, and fruit which is softening up will lose its stem naturally.

Ripening:
Leave fruit on counter out of the sun.

To hasten ripening:
Put the avocado in a brown paper bag and close tightly.

Not fast enough?:
Add an overripe apple or banana to the bag before closing tightly.

Still not fast enough?:

Place the closed bag with the overripe apple or banana (and of course the avocado) in the sun or warm spot of about 80°.

Fruit, as it ripens, gives off ethylene gas which in turn hastens the ripening of the fruit around it. Hence the expression "One rotten apple spoils the barrel". One customer has told me that the banana skin itself does the job for her which is more economical than using the whole fruit.

I once had to fill a large order for a hospital and was desperate to get enough ripe fruit at one time. That led to experimenting and the recommendations I give above. I also learned that citrus cannot substitute for the apple or banana.

I had heard that burying the avocado in flour would ripen it in a day or two so I experimented but had absolutely no success with that method.

RECIPES

Audrey Ovington is the owner of the Cold Spring Tavern in the Santa Ynez area. It is well known for its weekend motorcyclist patrons and equally well known for its gourmet dining in the evening. From Audrey comes the following recipe and, in her own words, the history behind it.

Salma-Cado

"Twenty-four or more years ago, in a little town outside of Osaka, Japan, the late Eunice Berry, a resident of Ojai, California, had dinner with an oriental friend of hers and he served her the first `Salma-Cado' that she had ever tasted. It was a creation of his own. By way of the fact that he was a chef in the city, she knew the dish would be tasty but it was even more delicious than she thought it would be. What she had not figured on was that `hot avocado' tasted like crab! It was a fantastic luncheon dish."

Audrey has served this dish "any number of times and it always brings raves". She featured it in her cookbook "The Barnholm Cook Book".

3 ripe avocados	1/3 cup tender celery, chopped fine
1/3 cup mayonnaise	4 1/2 oz. can tiny shrimp (rinse and drain)
1/2 cup sour cream	
1/4 teaspoon seasoned salt	4 3/4 oz. can red salmon (drain and flake)
sprinkling of celery salt	

Cut avocados in half. Remove seeds. Mix all other ingredients. Fill holes in avocados and completely cover top, mounding it up. Put dab of sour cream on top. Broil slowly until good and hot. Eat out of shell.

Serves 6

The following recipe comes from "The Avocado Lover's Cookbook" written by Joyce Carlisle. This particular recipe is one of her favorites.

STEAK TOSTADAS

with Avocado Salsa

Preparation time: 35 minutes, plus 2 hours marinating time

Yield: 4 servings

> 1/4 c water
>
> 3 T Dijon style mustard (1 T dried, ground mustard)
>
> 2 T cooking oil
>
> 1 T soy sauce
>
> 2 lbs. round steak
>
> 8 corn tortillas, cooked crisp
>
> 2 c sour cream

Combine for marinade: water, mustard, oil, and soy sauce. Score meat on both sides and marinate for 2 hours, turning frequently. Drain meat, reserving marinade. Grill or broil meat to taste. Baste while cooking. Carve meat into strips and place on tortillas. Spoon remaining marinade over. Top with avocado salsa and sour cream.

Avocado Salsa

1 avocado, diced

1 tomato, diced

1 4 oz. can green chiles

1 T sliced scallion

1 T cilantro, stemmed

1/2 t cumin seed

salt to taste

Toss together all ingredients. Chill.

NOTES

BERRIES

Berries. They bring back memories for me of those childhood days on our Vermont farm. In June when the wild strawberries ripened, my mother, three brothers, one sister and I would collect berry pails (lard buckets with bail handles which could hang from our belts) and climb the slope to the best patches we could find.

Chandler strawberry

Not one of the big hybrid strawberries at our markets could begin to compare to the wild strawberries we gathered. They were tiny little things a quarter to half inch long but they were bursting with flavor and sweetness. I have this notion that there is just so much flavor and sweetness allotted to each berry and the larger the berry, the more it is spread out, the smaller the berry, the more concentrated it is.

We picked until we had enough to make a shortcake large enough for seven big appetites. Mother would do the tedious job of hulling with nary a complaint or sigh, then make two thick 9" round biscuit shortcakes which were each cut in half crosswise to make a four layer shortcake. The topping was freshly whipped cream from our own cow. Our whole dinner consisted of this one magnificent creation.

We picked wild blueberries, wild blackberries, wild red raspberries and wild black raspberries. I think those last were my favorite kind. Aaahh.

General Information

There are many varieties of berries at our markets and they share certain traits.

1. They are all very fragile with the exception of blueberries.

2. The color should be very deep and rich.

3. They do not ripen further after picking.

Selecting

It is very difficult to pick each berry at the prime moment so berries in any given basket will vary from perfect to just a bit under ripe. But do look for overall good color with as many deeply colored berries as possible.

Using

They should have been picked just prior to market or the night before if you have a very early morning market. Generally use them the day you buy them. The most fragile berries, blackberries and raspberries, have a way of developing a fur coat when put in the refrigerator overnight or even when left on the counter. Strawberries are more durable but need to be refrigerated if not used the day of purchase.

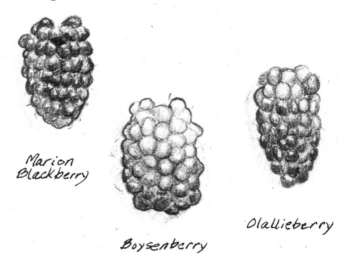

Marion Blackberry

Boysenberry

Olallieberry

It is best not to wash any of the blackberries or raspberries because of their fragility. Pick out by hand any stray hay seeds or leaf particles which may be in them. If you feel they need to be washed, do so at the last minute before using them.

Strawberries may be washed carefully. Place in a basin of water and gently swish, then scoop out and drain in a colander.

Varieties and Characteristics

Blackberries

Early summer to early fall. There are many varieties to extend the season and they are usually known by their varietal name (i.e. boysenberry). Most of them grow on thorny canes and the core remains in the berry when picked.

The ones we refer to simply as *"blackberries"* are late summer berries. These berries can be quite tart if they are not fully ripe so look for very dark berries. Sometimes there will be individual nodules of red on an otherwise black berry. Avoid these if you can though a few in the basket won't make a big difference.

My husband and I raise these berries in a hybrid gone wild. We understand that the plants were pulled up and thrown over the bank some years before we purchased the property. They took hold and serve as excellent erosion control but are in an impossible tangle so we do not fertilize or water and the berries are smaller than hybrids but oh, so much sweeter and more flavorful! You might want to check growers for the possibility of such "wild" berries at your market.

Boysenberries: Early summer. These are a specific variety of blackberry which are dark purple. They become dull when ripe due to a "bloom" and have the same tendency toward red tart nodules on otherwise ripe berries.

Raspberry

Olallieberries: Early summer, starting before boysenberries and overlapping with them. Another variety of blackberry which is shiny, black, and long.

Raspberries

These berries are closely related to blackberries, almost always growing on thorny canes. However, these berries pull off the core when picked, making them look like little caps.

Raspberries, red: Late spring through late fall. There are many different varieties which extend the season over a long period of time. Some varieties have both a spring and fall crop from the same plants. They have a "bloom" or dusty look to them.

Raspberries, golden: Available in mid to late summer and fall. These raspberries are more difficult to raise in California and vines are not as productive as the red so they are not commonly found at our markets. If you find them, try them for a nice change and take advantage of their beautiful color in your company dishes.

Hybrid

Tayberries: Late spring. These are a cross between red raspberries and blackberries which got its name from the Tay River in Scotland where they were developed. The flavor is not especially good but they do make good pies and preserves. The stem often clings to the berry and they are larger than Olallieberries.

Strawberries

With a combination of cultural practices and hybrids, strawberries are now available year round. There are numerous varieties, the most common of which are Chandler and Oso Grande but look for other smaller and less common varieties.

Ideally, the berry should not be picked until full maturity and will be solid red from stem to tip. Often, however, the berries are picked before full maturity (more durable) and often are white at the stem end. This white area should not have hints of green. Also, this white end will have virtually no flavor.

The quality of the fruit depends on

Pasero Strawberry

weather, farming methods, and maturity at harvest as well as variety. This means that the same variety of berries from the same grower can vary throughout the year, so the best way to find high quality berries is to ask the grower for a sample.

Sometimes you will find strawberries with the stems attached. The stem has no bearing on quality or durability. They are very attractive and ideal for special uses like dipping in chocolate or topping a dessert. Keep in mind that you will have fewer berries in a basket when the stems are attached.

Occasionally you may find a grower who sells seconds, berries which have unusual shapes or which need to be used right away. They will be considerably less expensive and if you are able to prepare them as soon as you get home, they can be an excellent buy, especially for jelly, jam, and syrup.

Blueberries

Summer. Blueberries are available only in limited areas of the state because of the growing conditions which they require. If your market has them, they will be available for about 6 to 7 weeks. These are the most hardy of the berries and have a much longer shelf life than the other berries described in this chapter.

Blueberries freeze well. Do not rinse. Put a layer of berries on a cookie sheet, flash freeze, and then bag or put into plastic containers.

Blueberry

CHERIMOYA

Cherimoya is a subtropical fruit and one of the newer introductions to our farmers' markets. This fruit is very expensive and *very* good! They are light green to yellowish green fruit shaped somewhat like a strawberry or pine cone, with markings which resemble thumbprints or scales. They may be quite smooth or have numerous bumps. The interior creamy flesh contains dark seeds about the size of beans.

Selecting

Firmness - Cherimoyas are fragile once they are ripe so they are picked while still firm. They are brought to market both firm and ready to eat. Firm ones will be easier to handle in your basket. However, if you want fruit ready to eat, simply handle it very gently, keeping it on top of your heavier purchases.

Color should be light green to yellowish green depending on variety. Avoid fruit which is darker green as it is not mature enough. Oftentimes there are dark areas on the skin which do not affect the quality.

Shape and **Size** have no bearing on quality. I have seen beautiful large symmetrical fruit of different varieties but most cherimoyas come in irregular and fascinating shapes and a wide range of sizes. Choose the fruit depending on your use, small for your first taste, huge if you have a passion for it, small for single serving, large for a family, unusual shape for conversation.

Stems, Cracks, and **Spoilage** - If the cherimoya does not have a stem attached and the fruit is split open at the stem end, look for brown discoloration inside the center of the fruit. If the fruit is ready to eat and shows only a small amount of this brown spoilage, you will lose very little. If the fruit is still hard and has spoilage, it will spread as the fruit ripens and there will be greater loss.

Cracks on the side of the fruit are easier to evaluate. If they are dried and healed, there will be no loss other than the surface. If the area is moist and softer than the

Cherimoya

rest of the fruit, that portion will have to be discarded.

Ripening
Let the fruit sit on your kitchen counter to soften. It will take only 3 to 5 days. Do not let it get overripe as it will lose its wonderful flavor and start to go bad very quickly. Spoilage is easily identified by light brown color in the creamy flesh.

Using
Although the skin of some varieties can be eaten, it is almost always discarded. Cut the fruit in half or into wedges and scoop the flesh out with a spoon, discarding the seeds as you go along.

Season
Winter through spring. They can appear as early as October and as late as mid June.

CITRUS

GENERAL INFORMATION

The following information holds true for all citrus and you will want to keep it in mind as you read about specific varieties.

The smoother the skin the thinner the skin for any given variety.

Citrus ripens only on the tree. Once picked it does not get any riper. If it is picked too soon and is tart it will remain tart.

Softness is not an indication of ripeness. It is an indication of how long the fruit has been picked. (Valencia oranges can begin to soften on the tree at the very *end* of their season.)

Softer fruit will release its juice more freely.

Ripe drops or windfalls are excellent in quality. Do not hesitate to buy them as long as they are in good condition. To test for condition, hold the fruit in the palm of your hand and feel the whole for consistency of texture. This technique will quickly identify any bruised or bad spot.

Juiciness is not determined by softness of fruit or thickness of skin. It is determined by variety of fruit, ripeness, and growing conditions.

There should never be any reason for a grower to add color to the skin of any citrus sold at a farmers' market. The time frame is so short from picking to customer that there is no need to pick underripe fruit, and educated consumers understand regreening. (See "ripeness" under oranges.)

ORANGES

Most oranges in the California markets will be **navel** or **Valencia**.

However, **blood oranges** are becoming more readily available and there are sometimes **seedling** oranges.

Seasons of navel and Valencia
Navels are available from approximately the beginning of the year to mid summer and Valencias from early summer to the end of the year. The supply at your particular market will vary depending upon where the grower comes from and upon the grower's picking patterns.

Fruit ripens sooner in a warmer locale so a San Diego navel will be ripe earlier in the season than a Fillmore navel. A Fillmore navel will be ripe sooner than a Santa Barbara navel. This stretches the season out for us very nicely. The timing of the pick by an individual grower also stretches the season in any particular area.

Commercial growers are forced to pick their fruit early while it is still underripe as it must go from orchard to packing house to grocery store and it sits between each of these stages. Tree-ripened fruit would be rotten long before it reached the consumer. Happily, the farmers' market gives the consumer a chance to buy tree-ripened oranges the day or day after they are picked.

The grower can start picking as early as the commercial growers or he can wait until the very end of the season. Get to know your orange growers, where they are from and what their season is. The longer the fruit is on the tree, the sweeter and juicier it is.

Navel Orange

If you have the choice of getting Valencias or navels in January, keep in mind that those uglier and softer Valencias are food for the gods. After all, they have been on the tree about a year and a half developing sweetness and juice. But if you are tired of juice oranges and think you just have to have a firm pulpy navel, go ahead and get it. Just keep in mind that it will be less tasty and sweet, probably even a little tart.

The reverse holds true at the other end of the season. In July, it is the navel that will be food for the gods and the Valencia that will be a bit short on flavor and juice and sweetness.

Ripeness
Look at the blossom end (bottom) of the fruit. That is the last part of the orange to change color as it ripens. There should be no green there. Valencias have a unique trait called "regreening". In hotter inland areas, the summer sun causes chlorophyll to return to the skins. This coloring is never on the bottom of the fruit and does not affect the quality of the fruit. I have actually seen a bit of this trait on navels as well.

Navel oranges are considered eating oranges because their pulp is firm and too much of it is wasted when the fruit is squeezed. Furthermore, the juice separates when it stands. There is no reason why they can't be squeezed as long as you understand their limitations. Simply drink the juice as soon as it is squeezed, which is best nutritional practice anyway.

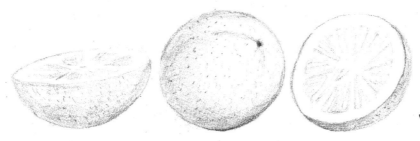

Valencia
Orange

Valencia oranges are well known as juice oranges. There is very little waste when these oranges are squeezed and the juice does not separate. Keep in mind that the half-life of vitamin C is one hour. This means that if you squeeze the orange one hour before serving the juice, half the vitamin C will already be lost. It is by far best to drink the juice immediately after squeezing. These oranges can easily be eaten in sections or cut in half crosswise and scooped out with a spoon like a grapefruit.

Blood oranges come in several different varieties, all of which ripen from approximately January through May, a shorter season than either navels or Valencias. Again, the actual time you find them in your market will depend upon the location of the grower and his picking philosophy.

Tarocco
Blood orange

The **Tarocco blood orange** has a very firm texture and varies from quite red in hotter interior valleys to very little or no red when grown along the coast. Even if there is no red, they are a unique and delicious orange well worth trying.

Moro blood oranges are probably the most commonly raised variety because they develop a beautiful red no matter where grown, though along the coast they may be a tad short on color at the stem end. They are not as flavorful as the Tarocco but are much more reliable for color.

Seedling oranges come in different shapes and sizes because the trees spring up from old root stock, many from the very early citrus groves of California. My husband and I have a number of these trees. Some resemble navels and ripen at the same time as navels but are full of seeds. Others have thick skins like navels but contain pulp like a Valencia and ripen at the same time as Valencias. You will need to rely on your grower for guidance in purchasing these fruit which are all excellent when tree ripened.

MANDARINS
(and TANGERINES)

For a delightful change from the common sweet oranges such as the navel and Valencia, you might want to try some of the many varieties of mandarin oranges. These oranges have long been raised in the Mediterranean, India and the Orient. They are becoming increasingly popular here, and both California and Florida have increased production.

The oranges in this group usually have skins which are easily removed and the segments are easily separated. Most varieties have a generous number of seeds but there are some with few or none.

There is often confusion about some of the names in this group. *Tangerines* are actually mandarins which have deeply colored orange-red peel. *Tangors* are a cross between mandarin and sweet orange. *Tangelos* are a cross between mandarin and grapefruit.

Selecting
It is not always easy to pick out the best fruit by looking and feeling so I would recommend taste testing as the most reliable way of selecting the best.

Color - the fruit should be mostly of a good orange or red-orange shade but some green is often present even when the fruit is ripe.

Tightness of skin - depending on the variety, the skin may be tight to the fruit or beginning to come away just a bit. Generally, if the skin is very loose and puffy feeling, the fruit has started to dry out.

Weight - look for a good weight to size ratio.

Season
It is possible for the early Satsuma variety to start showing up at the market in late November. Other varieties will start appearing in December and throughout the following months with the season ending in mid-summer.

GRAPEFRUIT

If you are looking for a grapefruit which is wonderfully juicy, sweet and flavorful all at once, you will have to go to Florida. California has numerous superb fruits but grapefruit are not among them. I must say, however, that new varieties are being developed and we are making progress!

Grapefruit need hot weather to be at their best which means that the fruit grown in the desert is sweeter than that grown along the coast. Coastal fruit needs to remain on the tree considerably longer than inland fruit which helps spread out the season for us.

Varieties

Marsh Seedless is a common white variety, which can be grown along the coast as well as in the hotter inland areas. The coastal grown are rather thick skinned and quite tart but have good flavor.

Ruby and Star Ruby are pink-fleshed varieties which, as far as I can tell, are raised only in the hotter areas of the state. They are considerably sweeter than the coastal grown Marsh but at the same time they have a less hearty flavor.

The University of California does extensive research in agriculture which benefits all of us. One of these benefits is the development of new grapefruit varieties which produce juicier, sweeter fruit.

Be on the lookout for Oro Blanco and Melo Gold.

Selecting

Color should be deep yellow. If you are getting a pink fleshed variety, the skin may have a red blush to it. Avoid any fruit which has a hint of green as it is underripe.

The heaviest fruit have the most pulp and juice.

Season

Summer is the peak of the season but if your market has fruit from different areas of the state, you may find desert grapefruit as early as January and coastal grapefruit well into the fall.

PUMMELOS

The botanical name for this fruit is *Citrus grandis* and it is indeed the largest of our citrus. Pummelos are sometimes called Chinese grapefruit and are quite similar to grapefruit. However, they are usually much larger, have much thicker skin, have a firmer texture, and are sweet. They come in both pink and white flesh varieties.

Selecting

The color should be a typical grapefruit yellow all over.

Weight in proportion to size is an indication of juiciness.

Season

Ranges from early in the year to early summer, depending upon variety and location of trees.

Using

Since pummelos are firm and the membranes much tougher than those in grapefruit, preparation is quite different than it is for grapefruit.

First, score the rind and remove as you do when fixing an orange. Next, break apart as you would an orange or make a cut from top to bottom and spread open. When you spread the fruit open, the center edge of the membrane on each section is likely to burst open. If it doesn't, use a knife to slice the center edge of the membrane. Peel this membrane back with fingers. Run your thumb under the pulp to pry it up. Because the pulp is so firm, this is quite easy to do without breaking it or spritzing juice around.

Eat it fresh or use it in salads where its firm texture holds up beautifully.

KUMQUATS

At the other end of the spectrum from pummelo are kumquats, the smallest of our citrus varieties. They are unique in that the whole fruit is eaten, skin and all. The skin is actually the sweet part of this fruit and the pulp is tart and juicy. They are small oval or round orange-colored fruit. The number of seeds depends on the variety.

Selection
Color is a good guide. Look for rich orange. However, if there are some fruit with pale color, they may be just as fine in quality. I have had fruit on the same tree vary in shade even when the fruit are all ripe. Regardless of the shade of orange, all the green should be gone.

Season
Winter into spring

Using
Roll the little fruit between your palms to soften it and break down the interior. Pop the whole thing into your mouth and eat it.

Kumquats are commonly used for preserves. They are also a very decorative fruit.

Kumquats

LEMONS

The most common lemon is the **Eureka**, found in the grocery store and the farmers' market year round. **Lisbon** variety may also be available but is usually not identified as such since it is so similar to the Eureka.

Shape and size
Since those in the store have gone through a packing house, only those that meet

standard shape and size requirements reach the store. At the farmers' market, there are no such requirements so you will find shapes which range from the typical oblong to round ones to crooked ones.

Sizes range from small walnut-sized fruit to huge grapefruit-sized fruit. The quality of the fruit is not determined by size or shape. Don't hesitate to get small lemons if you need only a small amount at a time as little ones are just as good as large ones. In fact, the giant lemons tend to have very thick skins.

Eureka lemon

Ripeness
The deeper the yellow, the riper the fruit. It is often picked when pale yellow, perhaps with a hint of green which is known as a silver. A fully tree-ripened fruit will be a rich yellow.

Do not confuse softness with ripeness. Color is an indication of ripeness. Softness is an indication of how long the fruit has been off the tree. Once picked, the lemon will not get any riper but it will become softer as it sits. The best flavor and most juice will be found in the ripest fruit and the juice will be most easily squeezed if the fruit is soft.

If you have only firm lemons on hand and need juice, put the lemon in the microwave on high for about 15 - 30 seconds depending on size. If you do not have a microwave, bruise the fruit by rolling it vigorously on your countertop.

Durability
The firmer the fruit, the longer it will keep. The softer it is, the shorter its shelf life but the easier it will be to extract all the juice. Firmer, greener lemons will keep at room temperature for several weeks. Soft ripe fruit may last only a matter of days at room temperature. Refrigeration will prolong the life in any case.

Selecting
A rich yellow smooth-skinned fruit is the sweetest and juiciest.

Appearance
Growers who don't spray will have fruit that looks less perfect than that in the grocery store. It may have pock marks on the skin. That tells you that our little friend the snail has been feasting. No harm done unless you want the lemon for decorative purposes.

Another problem for the grower is red scale, which is a tiny insect which looks like little reddish dots on the skin. This creature is not a problem to the cook. If you

Meyer lemon

wish to use only the juice, ignore the little things and squeeze away. If you want the skin for zest or decorative purposes, get a little brush and scrub the dots away.

A less common lemon is the **Meyer**. It is a smoother skinned, rounder, more orangey yellow fruit than the Eureka. It is also much less acid and therefore sweeter than the Eureka. There are people who like to eat them the same way they eat oranges, but, as sweet as they are for a lemon, they are still a bit too tart for most of us to eat plain.

Season

The peak crop comes in during the winter. Theoretically, they are available year round, but currently there are not enough growers raising them in different climate zones for this to be the reality. As customers request them more and inspire growers to raise them, they should be available much like limes are with the abundance in winter and lesser quantities throughout the rest of the year.

Sungold and **pink fleshed** lemons are even less common than Meyer but are interesting varieties. Both have variegated striping on the skin when underripe which makes them attractive fruit for display. The Sungold skin becomes solid yellow when ripe and the pink fleshed becomes solid orange but both retain the slight ridges that are so prominent when underripe.

They can be used in place of Eureka lemons.

RECIPES
Meyer Lemon Salad Dressing

1/4 c Meyer lemon juice

2 t sugar

1/2 c canola oil

Mix all ingredients and shake well. This dressing enhances the flavors of the vegetables in your salad.

The following cake is out of this world. Butter can be used instead of margarine and the cake will be creamy white instead of yellow.

Meyer Lemon Cake

1/2 pound margarine	3 c sifted flour
1 3/4 c sugar	1/2 t baking soda
3 eggs	2 T Meyer lemon juice
1 c buttermilk	2 T Meyer lemon zest

Cream margarine and sugar. Add eggs, one at a time, mixing well after each addition. Mix flour and soda together and add alternately with milk, starting and ending with flour. Add lemon juice and zest last, stirring only enough to mix well.

66

Pour into 10″ greased tube pan and bake at 325° for 1 hr. 5 min. or until done. While cake is baking prepare topping.

Topping

| 1 3/4 c confectioners sugar | 1/2 c Meyer lemon juice |
| 1/2 c margarine | 3 T Meyer lemon zest |

Sift sugar and, using microwave-safe bowl, cream into margarine. Gradually add lemon juice and zest. The mixture will separate a bit because of the butter sugar ratio. Just before putting on cake, place in microwave and heat just until mixture evens out. (This can be done in a pan on the stove top if you don't have a microwave.)

After removing cake from oven, let cool about ten minutes and then remove from pan, inverting onto 12 or 14 inch plate. A tube pan with a removable bottom eases this step. Spoon warm topping over top of hot cake and dribble down sides and inside center. Cake can be eaten warm or cool.

LIMES

Limes in the grocery store are green and shiny and firm or at least were when they left the tree. But since that picking was many weeks ago, they are more often wizened by the time you find them. These limes are usually the somewhat round Mexican variety but they may be the more elongated Bearss lime, commonly grown here in California.

At farmers' markets the limes are most apt to be **Bearss** (rhymes with "scarce"). They are thin-skinned, almost seedless, very juicy, and beautiful yellow when ripe. Because limes are always green in the grocery store, (ripe fruit does not have a long enough shelf life to survive all the steps from harvest to supermarket) most people are under the misconception that ripe limes are green. But all limes are yellow when allowed to ripen on the tree.

Bearss Lime

In the winter when lime trees have their largest crop, I take baskets full of magnificent yellow fruit to market. Routinely, I have customers select their "lemons" out of my lime baskets so I now put bold "lime" signs in the baskets of limes.

How do you tell a ripe lime from a lemon? I have no trouble because I've worked with them for many years but I find I have some difficulty pointing out the difference to my customers. The lime is a more greenish yellow and the ripe lemon is a deeper yellow. But the lemon which is underripe is greenish yellow so color may not be the best way for a novice to tell the difference.

The stem end of a lime is usually puckered and the blossom end has just a tiny point. The tip on the blossom end of a lemon tends to be larger. Generally, the lime is a more symmetrical fruit and the lemon is uneven. The lime is smoother and thinner skinned. If you still can't figure it out, the easy solution is to put the fruit in different bags!

Season
Limes are available year round. However, the main crop comes in mid-winter with smaller crops the rest of the year. During the peak, you should find quantities of nice ripe yellow limes. Limes can, of course, be used green and during some parts of the year they may be available only in their unripe green stage. Don't hesitate to use them then but know that the ripe yellow ones when in season are sweetest and best.

Selecting
Limes that have dropped off the tree and been gathered by the grower are perfectly acceptable. It is very easy to judge the quality of a lime by looking at it and feeling it. Hold the fruit in the palm of your hand so you can feel the whole. It should be uniformly firm or soft.

Keep an eye out for spoilage at the blossom end which will appear translucent and feel too soft. If a grower is selling this kind of fruit at a discount, it can be a very good buy since the damage is limited to exactly what you see.

Keeping quality
The firmer the fruit, the longer it will keep. The softer it is, the shorter its shelf life, but the easier it will be to extract all the juice. If you discover that you have a piece of fruit with the start of spoilage at the blossom end, just cut that portion off and use the rest.

RECIPES

Compared to lemons, Bearss limes need only half the amount of sugar to sweeten.

Bearss Limeade
1 1/2 T lime juice from ripe Bearss limes

2 t sugar

3/4 c water

Stir sugar in lime juice until dissolved. Add water. Makes one serving.

Bearss Lime Juice

If you love ripe lime juice, purchase a large quantity when the fruit is at its peak and prices are at their lowest. Squeeze and freeze in cubes or measured amounts, depending upon your planned use.

Serving suggestion: add frozen juice cubes to sparkle water or plain water.

NOTES

DATES

I usually keep a supply of fresh dates on hand to help satisfy my sweet tooth. On a camping trip to Oregon a few years ago, I got a craving for dates so we went to the supermarket where I bought a tub of them. I sank my teeth into one, prepared for the wonderful fresh flavor I was accustomed to from my farmers' market dates. What a disappointment!! They surely renewed my appreciation of the farmers' market produce.

The Raising of Dates

Until I started writing this book, I had given little thought to the raising of dates, apparently satisfied that they grew on date palms. I had driven though a desert area where they are grown and had seen ladders attached to each very tall tree. I knew there were different varieties to choose from at the market. I suppose I thought that they simply grew until maturity when the farmer would climb the ladder and pick them in much the same way that I pick grapes in ripe bunches.

What a surprise I was in for when I talked to Robert Lower of Thermal, to learn all the steps he must go through before he can bring those delicious dates to us at the market.

For about two and a half years after completing school, Robert took odd jobs and ventured half way round the world. His travels took him to northern Africa and the Mediterranean where he became greatly interested in dates, not the horticulture, but simply the varieties, uses, and the role they play in that part of the world.

Not until he returned to the States and took a trip to Mexico did he become interested in the raising of dates. It was on this trip to Mexico that he stayed overnight in an abandoned date grove in Indio. On the way back from Mexico, he stopped again in Indio to see what he could learn about this abandoned grove.

It turned out to be in the ownership of Zane Grey's daughter. The chimney and foundation of an old structure which he had seen proved to be the remnants of an old cabin where Zane Grey did much of his writing.

Robert made arrangements to lease the property and so in the fall of 1973 started his adventure with organic date horticulture. He has raised them ever since. In 1979 he bought his own place, Flying Disc Ranch, in Thermal, where he raises the dates which he sells at a number of our markets. Here is what I learned from him.

Palm trees are propagated by root suckers cut from mother or father palms. It takes approximately ten years from the time the sucker is planted to the time the tree is ready to bear fruit.

Then begins much ladder climbing. The female blossoms are dry, they have no nectar, so the bees ignore them. But the male blossoms are "paradise" for bees says Robert because they are dense and rich and a bee can gather a full load in no time at all. He wastes no time at the female blossoms. That means the bees are of no help in pollinating. Natural pollination depends on the wind which results in perhaps a 15% pollination rate, hardly satisfactory for growers who are making a living from their dates.

When the male flowers, which are usually tied to prevent them from bursting, open, they are picked, shaken to remove all the mature pollen, and hung for several days after which they are shaken again for more pollen.

Next, the pollen is carried up the female tree where the blossoms are hand pollinated, a procedure done two times.

Now there is a one and one half month wait while the full extension of the bunch is realized. Time to climb up the tree again and tie the bunch down to a lower branch for support because by the time the fruit is mature, the bunch can easily weigh 35 pounds and even as much as 50 to 75 pounds.

Approximately a month after this step, a worker climbs up the tree and works suspended in a saddle cutting off low fronds which are in the way of the fruit which is at this time in a green or "kimry" stage. Manilla paper is then wrapped around each bunch, tied at the top and stapled down the side. This open-bottomed cone protects the fruit from birds and direct rainfall.

During August and September the fruit remains protected as it grows into the yellow, red or purple "kahlal" stage. At this time the fruit has its highest moisture content even though it is still firm.

The next stage of growth is called "tamar" when the dates become very soft and start developing the darker color they will have when mature. They can be harvested at this time but are very difficult to handle because of their softness. They can't be washed or handled beyond simply picking and placing in a box.

The final stage is cured ripe when the fruit has the familiar look and texture we associate with dates.

Harvesting
The grower keeps an eye on the ripening progress. Harvest time depends on the variety of date and the type of farming procedures used. Robert is an organic grower so he starts harvesting Medjool dates when only about 10% of the bunch has reached the ripe stage since this variety is prone to insect infestation which can cause the fruit to ferment. He cleans the bunch out, taking only the ripe dates and repeats this three to five times a month. Other varieties are harvested when greater percentages of fruit are ripe.

Harvesting starts in late August with the kahlal Barhi, then into September with the Medjool. By October most varieties are ready so it is a busy time. The season ends with the harvest of the Deglet Noor and the late Barhi.

When the bunch is picked, the mature fruit is removed, washed, sorted, and packed. The fruit still in the kahlal stage is placed on a rack to finish drying (about five days).

The fruit is all washed and then frozen at least 72 hours to kill any insects. At last it is ready for market after what I figure is a minimum of seven trips up the ladder of each tree. I am very thankful there are people who don't have the fear of heights that I have. If we were dependant on me for dates, I'm afraid we would be deprived of this delicious fruit.

Availability
The foregoing harvest information tells you when the new crop is in. But dates are available all year since they store well. Not all varieties will always be available. Nevertheless, you should have a choice all year.

Quality
Dates are hand sorted and almost every one is individually handled. They are graded by size, moisture, and appearance. Robert explained that the number of grades varies from one variety to another. For instance, Medjool comes in bonus, choice, large, select, fancy, and jumbo. The Deglet Noor has about fifteen grades. As long as you like the dates you get, don't worry about the grading.

Nutrition note for diabetics
All dates contain sugar but the form varies. Most have invert sugar (like honey). The Medjool has complex sugar. Some are suitable for diabetic diets but others are not. If you are a diabetic, you might want to check with your physician or a nutritionist regarding which dates you can have in your diet.

Storage
The drier the date variety the longer it will keep in your cupboard. Moister ones can ferment if they sit out, especially in warm weather, because the fresh dates we get at our farmers' markets have no preservatives. It is best to put them well wrapped in your refrigerator or, for longer storage, put them in the freezer. If sugar crystals appear on the exterior of the fruit, don't worry. This is normal and does not alter the quality or flavor.

Varieties
In reality there are thousands of varieties of dates because they are not true to seed. In order to get true varieties, a grower propagates his trees from shoots of existing trees.

The most common at our farmers' markets are:

Barhi - a small roundish date, very sweet and almost honey flavored. This is one of the most interesting varieties because it can be sold in the kahlal stage. When sold this way the dates are still on the stem. During August, September, and October they are sold fresh. Take them home and leave them on your counter to ripen, which they do one or two at a time, changing from the light yellow firm to light brown very soft. Pluck them and eat them right from the stem. From October to July they are sold

Zahidi date

frozen (to preserve them). By the time you get frozen ones they may have thawed and will all ripen at the same time.

Dayri - This date is red in its kahlal stage and looks very dark purple in the sunlight when ripe. It is an excellent keeper.

Deglet noor - This date is the most common commercially grown date because it is hardy, versatile and easy to raise.

Medjool - a large, plump very creamy date, perhaps the most prized for eating fresh. It is also the most expensive of the varieties.

Variations

Extruded - Dates are put through a macerator which removes the pits and stem ends (at least most of them!) and produces 3/8 inch diameter strips. These strips are treated two ways.

1. They are dipped in confectioner's sugar or oat flour and broken into short pieces. In this version they are good nibblers and a real time saver for the baker. I use them in my date nut breads. The one draw back to them in baking is that the date is very fine throughout the batter, with no meaty chunks to bite into or look pretty, but the flavor is not in the least compromised.

2. The strips are put through a grinder which sends the date out in a long bar shape which is cut and rolled in coconut. These bars can be served like candy or can be used in cooking.

Dehydrated - Dates look and act as if they are a dried fruit but in reality they are simply a ripe fruit which handles very much like a dried fruit. They can, however, be dried and stored in an airtight container for a long period of time. Dehydrated dates are sold in a somewhat granular form and can be used in baking or sprinkled on top of desserts and hot cereal.

Medjool Date

History

Dates are thought to be the oldest cultivated crop in the civilized world and there is a great deal of history and folklore surrounding them. Look in Section V for some interesting books to read about dates.

RECIPE

My sister, Judith Reynolds, is allergic not only to sugar but also to the favorite substitutes, honey and molasses. Unfortunately, when she developed the allergy, she didn't lose her sweet tooth, so she and I experiment with fruit-sweetened desserts and jams to satisfy that sweet tooth. All of our California dried fruits and dates make this challenge rewarding.

The following recipe is one she has developed. Not only does it not have sugar, but it also eliminates fat and cholesterol. And the best part is that it tastes yummy.

Date Raisin Bars

Blend in food processor:

     1 c unsweetened applesauce

     2 egg whites

     2 t vanilla

Mix together in separate bowl:

     1 c whole grain pastry flour

     2 t baking powder

Sprinkle half the flour mixture over mixture in processor.

Add: 8 oz. dates cut into thirds

     4 oz. raisins

Sprinkle remaining flour mixture over dried fruit.

Blend until well mixed and dates and raisins are chopped.

Put in 8" square pan sprayed with Pam. Bake at 350° for 30 minutes. Cut into squares. Makes 16 bars.

Judith Reynolds

NOTES

FEIJOA

also known as Pineapple Guava

I have two old large unpruned feijoa bushes and I know it is fall when I discover the first fruit dropped to the ground. I crawl around under the branches and even over one old branch that reaches out sideways. There are the remnants of a woodpile stacked many years ago between the bushes so there is a wonderful dampness and earthiness to revel in as I gather the fruit. I'm quite sure it reminds me of a true New England woods and that's why I love it.

No one seems sure how to pronounce the correct name for this fruit so we take the safe way out by using its alternate and very easy to pronounce name, pineapple guava. According to the *New Pronouncing Dictionary of Plant Names* put out by the Florists' Publishing Company, *fei* is pronounced either *fay* or *fee*. The *jo* is pronounced like the name *Joe*. The *a* is short like the *a* at the end of *banana*. The accent is on the middle syllable. *Fay joe' a* or *Fee joe' a*. It turns out to be as easy as pineapple guava and a lot shorter. (Some Israeli customers of mine told me that the name of this fruit in Israel is pronounced *fee joy' a*.)

Now that we can pronounce it, we should go ahead and use the proper name because this fruit is not a guava! It is in a different family altogether.

Feijoa

Season - October and November

Description
Feijoa are a very aromatic green elongated fruit with a very distinct blossom end and somewhat bumpy skin. They are never picked. Rather they are gathered from the ground after dropping from the bush. They are always hard when first gathered as is true of so many of our sub-tropical fruits.

The old varieties range in size from about half the size of a walnut to about 2 1/2 inches long. The new varieties are hybrids developed for their very large size.

How to select the fruit
Hard newly gathered fruit will keep up to two or three weeks without refrigeration before needing to be used. You will want to make sure you don't let it get overripe as it will turn brown inside. (You can still eat the fruit when it gets brown but it

doesn't look as nice.) It is ready to eat when it gets just barely soft. The softer the fruit the shorter the shelf life. How soon you will want to use it is one factor in choosing your fruit.

The other factor is what you plan to do with it. For eating fresh, the large ones are more practical. They also make an attractive addition to a fruit bowl arrangement. If you want to do preserving or glazing, the small ones work especially well. I find that the older small varieties seem to be a tiny bit sweeter and more flavorful than the new large hybrids.

How to eat fresh
Some people like to eat the whole thing except for the remnants of the blossom at the end.

However, many people find the skin a little too strong and they prefer to cut the fruit in half lengthwise and scoop out the soft insides with a spoon.

Other uses
Since this fruit is so fragrant, a bowlful on your table will fill your room with a delightful aroma.

Do not confuse recipes for true guava with recipes for feijoa as they are very different fruits. Since I grow this particular fruit I have experimented and developed some recipes of my own which follow.

RECIPES

Feijoa Pineapple Conserve
4 c sliced or mashed feijoa (approx. 1 1/2 lbs. fresh)

1/4 - 1/2 c lemon juice

2 c crushed pineapple with juice - unsweetened

1/2 c raisins

2 c sugar

To prepare feijoa, remove blossom end but do not peel.

In large kettle, cook feijoa, lemon juice, and pineapple until feijoa is softened. Add raisins and sugar. Boil until thick. (At first sign of sheeting, remove from heat.)

Pour into sterilized jars. Seal.

Yield: 5 half pints.

Conserve variations

Add 1/2 c walnuts with the raisins.

Add 1 c unsweetened applesauce with the feijoa and pineapple.

Glazed Feijoa I

Remove blossom end and thinly peel very small fruit. Place in saucepan with enough sugar and water to just cover fruit.

Use 3/4 c sugar to each 1/2 c water

Simmer, stirring occasionally, until feijoa is soft and syrup is thick, approx. 20 minutes.

Serving ideas for glazed feijoa:

Add to fruit salad

Use as garnish for meat

Use as topping on pound cake or sponge cake

Use as topping for ice cream

Glazed Feijoa II

Using very small fruit, remove blossom end but do not peel. Place in saucepan with enough sugar and water to just cover fruit.

Use 1/2 c sugar to each 1/2 c water

Simmer, stirring occasionally, until feijoa is soft and syrup thickened, approx. 40 minutes.

This version has a much heartier flavor which is quite different from the peeled version.

Fruit Breads

Substitute feijoa pulp for all or part of the fruit in any recipe such as banana bread.

Drying

My own attempt at drying this fruit was unsuccessful. I did not peel the fruit and apparently I overdried it. A customer of mine says she has good luck and this is her method. Peel the fruit and cut into thick slices. Remove from dryer after most of the moisture has evaporated but the fruit is still pliable.

NOTES

FIGS

One of the most common questions asked about figs is "Why are they so expensive?"

A major reason is **animals**. Birds love figs, ants love figs, and tiny little beetle-like insects love figs. Birds, scrub jays in particular, like to swoop into the trees and sample the fruit before it is quite ripe, leaving gaping holes in the side. Ants and beetles love to invade the interior of the almost-ripe fruit where the sweet juice attracts them.

Some fig varieties are more attractive to these animals than other varieties. I think the Brown Turkey fig is a favorite of theirs and I have a constant race to beat them to the fruit.

The net result is that the farmer can lose a fair amount of his crop and invest much time in trying to get there first each day!

The other major reason figs are expensive is that they are a **fragile** fruit.

Different varieties are less fragile than others and again, I think Brown Turkey is one of the most fragile. My husband and I have planted three other kinds of figs now which seem to be less fragile. I am telling the birds to stay with the Brown Turkey in hopes they will not discover the other varieties!

Figs do not travel and store well in their fresh state which explains why all those in the supermarkets are canned or dried. They must be picked every day or two as they shouldn't be picked until the neck starts to wilt and the fruit droops. If picked even a day sooner than this, they will have a milky fluid at the stem. Those picked a day or two early are fine for eating but are not at their scrumptious best.

Season
Mid or late summer through fall. Unpruned trees can yield an early or midsummer crop as well and these fruit are apt to be quite large.

Varieties
There are numerous varieties which vary in size, color, and durability. Here are a few of the more common ones.

Black Mission - a medium size dark fig with good keeping quality. Can be eaten fresh or dried.

Kadota - a medium size light green fig, roundish in shape for eating fresh. This variety is canned commercially but home canning is not recommended as the fruit tends to become mushy.

Brown Turkey - a large, moist, dark purple fig for eating fresh only.

Osborn - medium size purplish-brown for eating fresh.

Look for some of the interesting old varieties which are not grown commercially and are brought to market by small growers like John Tapia. His family has been living in Santa Barbara for six generations, and he has been coming to the local market since its beginning, bringing unusual varieties of various fruits.

John is supervisor of edible horticulture at the Santa Barbara Fair & Expo, a project which keeps him busy all year. He encourages growers to enter produce in the fair and he designs a beautiful display around the theme of farming. He is familiar with many old fruit varieties. He raises Strawberry figs, Conderas figs and Asiatic figs. He also brings to market non-commercial varieties of other fruit, such as Nabal avocados.

Selecting

Figs should feel plump and moist when you hold them in your hand. Be sure to handle them very carefully.

If they have a lighter, drier feel to them they will be less good. I believe the drier figs which one sometimes finds at the market during the height of the season are the result of too little irrigation water. It could also be that they were picked too early. Drier figs at the end of the season are the norm.

During low rainfall years, I have more figs which feel somewhat dry even though they have reached maturity. They are definitely less good than the moist ones, but still have the good fig flavor.

Color is another good indicator of quality in many varieties. Look for rich coloring.

Size is irrelevant to quality. End of the season fruit will be smaller.

Using

Figs are ripe when you buy them and ready to eat. The plumper and moister they feel, the sooner you should eat them. The drier ones will keep longer.

Eating fresh - Some people peel their figs before eating them but there is no reason that I know of to do this. It seems a pity to throw away so much good fruit. I always eat them whole, discarding only the last little bit of stem.

Freezing - Figs freeze well and can be prepared three basic ways.

Plain: Pack washed figs snugly in freezer container.

Sugar pack: Roll figs in sugar and place in freezer container or sprinkle sugar on figs as you layer them. When using a sugar pack, allow the sugar to dissolve before placing the packages in the freezer.

Syrup pack: Place figs in freezer container and cover with sugar syrup made with 2 1/2 c sugar to 1 qt. water. You can add 1/2 c lemon juice to each quart of syrup.

RECIPES

Pearl Farman's Sour Cream Fig Pie

This recipe comes to me by way of Pearl's daughter Nancy and Julie Porter who wait on tables at R & J's Panhandler Restaurant in the very small New Hampshire village of Charlestown. Rick and Jan, who own the restaurant and the people who work for them were so very kind to my aging parents that I sent them a thank you package of California produce. Included was a package of dried Black Mission figs which led them to the making and serving of this pie.

Mix together:

    1 c sugar

    1 egg

    1/2 c chopped dried figs (raisins can be substituted for figs)

    1 T flour

Add:

    1/4 t salt

    1 t vanilla

    1 c sour cream

Blend until smooth. Place in pie tin lined with standard pastry crust. Top with lattice-work crust. Bake at 450° for 10 minutes. Turn heat down to 350° and continue baking for 30 more minutes or until mixture doesn't adhere to knife.

John Tapia's Fig Jam

    3/4 c water

    4 1/2 c peeled fresh figs

    3/4 c lemon juice

    9 c sugar (or less if desired)

    1 box pectin

Place water and figs in large kettle and bring to boil. Add lemon juice, sugar, and pectin. Bring to full boil and cook for 3 minutes. Or follow method recommended on pectin box. Skim and pour into hot, sterilized jars. Seal.

Fig Conserve

5 1/2 c chopped fresh figs

2 c sugar

3/4 c lemon juice with pulp

3/4 c Thompson seedless raisins

3/4 c walnuts

Mix all ingredients and bring to boil. Cook until thickened. Pour into hot sterilized jars and seal at once. Yield: 6 cups.

Fig Apple Conserve

5 c chopped fresh figs

2 c chopped tart apple (8 oz. prepared)

2 c sugar

1/4 c lemon juice with pulp

1/2 c Thompson seedless raisins

Mix all ingredients and bring to boil. Cook until thickened. Pour into hot sterilized jars and seal at once. Yield: 5 - 5 1/2 cups.

GRAPES

Ruby and Bill Wilson of Pixley and Scott Peacock of Dinuba were very generous with their time and information for this chapter on grapes. In the stone fruit chapter, I share with you my visit to the Wilsons. Here I will introduce you to Scott and Linda and their family.

I have a lasting impression of them from Farm Conference '90 where I observed a family which included four daughters, ranging from high school to college age, each going to different workshops throughout the two days. I was immensely impressed that the whole family was so involved in the family business. I also was impressed with the knowledge that these young women had and the intelligent questions they asked at the workshops.

This is a family which truly practices family farming. Scott, who has a degree in agriculture, and Linda are both third generation farmers. Their grandfathers started farming in the Visalia and Fresno areas and they live in a house built by Linda's grandfather.

They farm fifty acres of deciduous fruit and grapes as well as some vegetables. Direct marketing at our California Farmers' Markets has enabled the Peacocks to maintain a strong small farm operation which in turn has nurtured family closeness, not always easy to come by in this era of mass child care programs and fifty-channel TV sets.

There are two basic kinds of grapes, those known as table grapes or **European grapes** (such as Thompson seedless) and those known as slip skin grapes or **American grapes** (such as Concord). There are also American hybrids which are a cross between the two types of grapes but are considered American since the slip skin trait is dominant.

TABLE GRAPES
They need a long very warm growing season so are raised in the inland valleys of California. These grapes may have seeds or not depending upon the variety.

Varieties
There are too many varieties to list but I will mention a few to give you a little idea of how they compare.

Flame - a seedless crisp grape

Ruby - a seedless grape, similar to Flame but later, smaller and less crisp

Ruby grapes

Centennial - white seedless, earlier and more elongated than Thompson seedless

Perlette - very early, less sweet and rounder than Thompson seedless

Season
Table grapes are available at our markets from early July, when Perlette appears, through early November, sometimes as late as the end of November.

Selecting
Avoid bunches that are too tight since they can have broken berries in the middle and may harbor mold and rot inside.

Perlette grapes

Color is important in judging the ripeness of grapes so you should select the richest colored bunches in any given variety. For instance, Thompson seedless grapes really should be turning yellow, almost a rosy yellow, if you want the very sweetest.

Size is a factor in selecting your grapes. Most grape growers use growth regulators (see Chapter 5 about grape horticulture) and this means that most grapes will be fairly large. With special treatment during growth, grapes can be encouraged to become very large and bring a high price. There is a trade off involved here. The larger grapes look lovely and are very easy to handle and use. However, they are not as sweet and flavorful as the smaller ones.

Using
These grapes are best eaten fresh.

Freezing: they can be frozen using a sugar water syrup or fruit juice to cover them in the freezer container.

Ruby and Bill Wilson remove the stems from Ruby variety grapes and freeze them whole without any syrup or juice. They eat them right from the freezer without thawing first which makes a delectable treat. They brought a container of them to the market one Saturday to give samples to customers and I had a chance to try them. They were delicious.

Drying: raisins all come from European grapes, mostly Thompson seedless but now we are finding Flame seedless raisins as well. You can dry your own. Be sure to get the very ripest fruit you can for drying.

If you live in a very dry sunny place you can sun dry your grapes. If you live along the coast and have a great deal of fog, you may have better luck using one of the dehydrators available on the market, using your oven, or building your own dryer. See Section V for information sources.

SLIP SKIN GRAPES

These grapes get their name from the fact that the skin slips off the pulp very easily. When you pinch the grape, the center pops out. They all have seeds.

These grapes have special memories for me and for some of my customers who come from back east. The climate there is far too cold for table grapes but we raised absolutely delicious Concord grapes and harvested them in the fall when the air was turning nippy and leaves were beginning to change color.

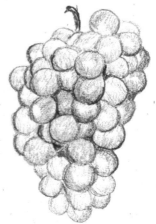

Happily these grapes grow quite nicely in the coastal areas of California, and my husband and I have some which we sell at our local market.

Season
Here in California these grapes ripen much earlier than they do back east. We harvest them in August and into early September depending on variety and location.

Concord grapes

Selecting
Color is the important guide to selecting these grapes. For example, Concord are very dark blue and should not have tinges of pink. Golden Muscat should be yellowish without distinct green.

Using
These grapes are delicious fresh. Pop the pulp out of the skin into your mouth and eat whole (seeds and all) or spit out the seeds. If you do not want to eat the skins, be sure to eat all of the interior of the skins as that is the very best part of this kind of grape.

RECIPES

Jelly and jam: These are the grapes to use for preserves.

Juice: Again, these are the grapes to use for making juice. There are two basic approaches.

1. You can heat to make juice flow and drain through a jelly bag which will give you pure very rich juice.

2. You can use the recipe my mother used which is very fast, easy, and gives far more beverage per pound of grapes.

Gladness Luce's Concord Grape Juice

Place 1 1/2c washed grapes, stems removed, in sterilized quart canning jar.

Add 1 c sugar

Fill to overflowing with **boiling** water and seal immediately. Shake to mix sugar, water and grapes.

Let stand for at least two weeks before serving.

Variation

One of my customers, Terry Helmick, prefers honey as a sweetener and uses 1/2 c honey in place of the sugar.

GUAVA

There are several kinds of true guava. (Keep in mind that "pineapple guava" is not guava but rather feijoa.)

Guava

Strawberry guava and Lemon guava are very similar except for their color as you might guess from their names. They are small round fruit that vary in size from very tiny up to slightly more than an inch in diameter. They have tiny hard round seeds throughout, very noticeable in the larger ones, less so in the smaller ones. This fruit grows on a bush which has some frost tolerance so it can grow in the cooler coastal areas.

Another true guava is the tropical guava which is a much larger fruit with pink pulp. It is a frost sensitive plant so cannot be grown in all areas. This is the guava that provides the juice for guava nectar in the grocery store. I have not been able to find any of this variety at our California Farmers' Markets.

Selecting
The fruit can be picked but the ripest fruit is that which has dropped or drops into one's hand with just the slightest nudge. Check with the grower selling the fruit to learn how he picks. Color is an indication of ripeness. Generally, the darker the color, the riper the fruit. Strawberry guava will be deep maroon and lemon guava will be rich yellow.

I don't know how to describe the flavor of this fruit and it is unusual so you might want to ask the grower if you can have a sample. Some people really don't care for the flavor at all but others develop a passion for it. I find it very hard to pick without helping myself to some of the choicest fruits on the bush! The very ripest are wonderfully sweet but many of the fruit do have a bit of tartness.

Using
This fruit is ready to eat as soon as it is picked. To eat fresh, just pop the whole thing into your mouth and eat it all. Don't worry about blossom end or seeds, though you shouldn't bite down too vigorously. Just enjoy. Very soft, richly colored fruit are the best and need to be eaten soon. Firmer fruit have a longer shelf life.

Besides eating fresh, you may want to try some of the following recipes. Genay Andre of Santa Barbara offered me the fruit from her bushes which have actually become slim graceful trees after many years of growth. She and Warren, a friend of hers, helped me pick several weeks in a row.

My own single bush did not offer me much opportunity to experiment but with Genay's generous offer, I spent those weeks working with more than 100 pounds of the strawberry guava and the following recipes are the result.

Season - fall

RECIPES

Juice Extraction

Wash and sort guava, discarding any spoiled fruit. Crush in single layers with potato masher. To each pound of fruit add 1/4 c water. Simmer 10 minutes, stirring frequently. Strain through jelly bag or 4 layers of cheesecloth resting in large colander. Yield: 1 pound guava gives approx. 1 c juice.

Puree Extraction

Wash, sort, and crush guava as for juice. There are several ways of extracting the puree, some easier than others.

I initially used a wooden spoon and a colander with small holes to extract the puree but found it very time consuming so went out and bought a large wire sieve. The job was done in a fraction of the time and actually yielded a slight bit more puree because some of the skin went through.

Then my mother passed on to me a Foley Food Mill which made the job very fast. I am sure there are electric appliances which would require less manual labor if you want to go to that expense or if you already have one.

Puree small amounts of crushed fruit at a time. Yield: 1 pound guava gives approx. 1 c puree.

An intensive taste test indicated that there was virtually no difference in the quality of the final product, regardless of the method used.

I also tested the results of puree made with only the ripest fruit and puree made with a blend of ripe and less ripe. Again, our taste tests indicated so little difference as to make it not worthwhile to do the extra sorting.

A VERY IMPORTANT NOTE about all of the guava jams and jellies that follow: Do not overcook. At the very first sign of sheeting, remove from stove. They jell further after cooling and sitting and I found that if I cooked them to the usual jelly stage, they became too solid to spread.

Regarding "sheeting" and jelling, *Joy of Cooking* by Rombauer and Becker has a nice explanation. Even with a jelly thermometer, this part of jelly and jam making is not an exact science. The more you practice, the better you will become, so don't get discouraged. Make notes for yourself about the characteristics of the individual fruits you work with to jog your memory the next season.

While we were picking, Genay and I reminisced about the guava jelly we remembered from childhood. Hers came in a wooden box and mine came in a large shallow metal tin. It was a rather solid block of jelly which we cut and ate in chunks. Our mouths watered just thinking about it. If you have such memories, you can easily make your own solid jelly by cooking these recipes to the usual temperature or jell stage. Genay found that my first batch of low sugar jam cooked the full time was very similar to the jelly of her childhood.

Guava Jelly

4 c guava juice

4 c sugar

2 T lime juice

Bring guava juice to boil and cook about one minute. Skim foam. I find that when I skim at this point it is easier and faster than leaving the whole job until the end of the cooking. Add sugar and lime juice. Boil rapidly, stirring, until jelly stage is reached. Skim if necessary, pour into hot sterilized jars and seal.
Yield: 5 cups

Low Sugar Guava Jelly

Follow recipe above except use only 2 1/2 c sugar.
Yield: 3 1/2 cups

Guava Syrup

2 c guava juice

2 1/2 c sugar

2 T lime juice

Bring guava juice to boil, add sugar and lime juice. Bring back to boil and cook only 45 seconds. Do not cook longer or you will have jelly because of the high sugar content.
Yield: 3 cups

Guava Jam

4 c guava puree

4 c sugar

2 T lime juice

Bring puree to boil, cook about one minute and skim. Add sugar and lime juice. Cook, stirring constantly, until thickened. Skim if necessary, pour into hot sterilized jars, and seal.
Yield: 5 cups

Low Sugar Guava Jam

2 1/2 c puree
1 1/2 c sugar
1 T lime juice

Cook as for guava jam above.
Yield: 2 cups

NOTE: In all of the jam and jelly recipes, lemon juice may be substituted for the lime juice. The result will be a more tart product.

Alice Pearce of Goleta makes many batches of strawberry guava juice and jelly in the fall. She shares with us her method of juice extraction and her jelly recipe, both of which are different from the ones above.

Alice Pearce's Strawberry Guava Juice

Remove flower end from guava and cut guava in quarters. In a large kettle, add 1 cup water for each pound of fruit. Bring to a boil. Reduce to simmer for 15-20 minutes. Strain through jelly bag or several thicknesses of cheese cloth. Do not squeeze bag.

This juice may be used just as it is for a beverage. It is also the juice she uses for the following jelly recipe.

Alice Pearce's Strawberry Guava Jelly

3 1/2 c strawberry guava juice (recipe above)
1/2 c lime or lemon juice (strained)
7 c sugar
1/2 bottle Certo (1 packet)
1 t butter (or margarine)

In a very large kettle, dissolve sugar in juices. Bring to rolling boil. Add Certo and 1 t butter to reduce foam and bring to full rolling boil that you can't stir down. Continue boiling for 1 minute. Remove from heat. Let foam settle and skim. Pour into hot sterilized jars and cover with hot paraffin.

Uncooked Guava Sauce

Guava sauce is quick and delicious. It can be eaten plain just as you eat applesauce.

To each cup uncooked puree, add 1/4 c sugar (or less if desired). Stir and let stand long enough for sugar to dissolve.

Cooked Guava Sauce

Cooking helps bring out a heartier guava flavor. Use 1/4 c sugar to each cup puree. Bring puree to boil and cook 2 minutes. Remove from heat, add sugar, and stir until sugar is dissolved.

Guava Yogurt

Add either uncooked or cooked guava sauce to plain nonfat yogurt for a scrumptious flavor not available in the ready-made flavors at the supermarket.

Guava Gelatin

1 pkg. plain gelatin
6 T sugar
1 c boiling water
1 1/2 c guava puree

Mix gelatin and sugar. Add boiling water and stir until gelatin is completely dissolved. Stir in guava puree. Refrigerate.

If you wish, you can whip this mixture when it begins to set. I like it whipped lightly with a wire whisk.

Fruit Shake

1 c guava puree
1 banana
1/4 c orange juice
6 ice cubes
1 c water or milk

Blend until ice is crushed and mixture is nicely whipped. Serve immediately in glasses.

Variations

Vary the proportions according to ingredients you have on hand.

Substitute ice cream or frozen yogurt for the ice and part of the water or milk.

Add a generous amount of chocolate syrup and this shake tastes remarkably like a raspberry truffle.

Guava Bread

1/2 c shortening	2 1/4 c flour
1 1/2 c sugar	1 t soda
2 eggs, slightly beaten	1 t cinnamon
1 1/2 c guava puree	1/2 t cloves
1 c raisins	

Cream shortening and sugar. Add eggs. Sift dry ingredients together and add alternately with puree. Add raisins last. Bake in large 9 1/4" loaf pan 1 hour at 350°.

NOTES

KIWI

Kiwi are the fuzzy brown oval fruit which have become very popular in recent years. The ones in the supermarket must fit preformed packaging so they are very uniform in size and shape. However, at the farmers' markets where there are no packaging constraints, you may find fruit as small as walnuts, and there are many "double" kiwis which can be quite large.

Kiwi are a fairly straightforward fruit when it comes to season and selection.

Selecting
Most fruit for sale are still hard and durable. Some growers bring ripe fruit which you should feel carefully as you do a ripe avocado or persimmon, placing the fruit in the palm of your hand and gently feeling the whole under only the slightest of pressure. It should feel evenly soft with no watery spots.

The finest kiwi are those which have been allowed to stay on the vine until they drop or at least have not been picked until the very end of the season. These are the most mature and therefore have the best flavor and sweetness. They can even be eaten hard as they have only a slight bit of tartness at this degree of maturity.

Obviously, we want to start eating kiwi earlier than the end of the season and large growers want to start harvesting earlier. It is important to let these early-harvest kiwi become soft before eating or they will be very sour.

All the first kiwi at the market will fall into this early-harvest category. Later in the season, if you want the very finest, you will have to ask the grower when he harvested, whether he has used cold storage or whether the fruit is fully vine-matured.

Season
This is a fall fruit which grows on a deciduous vine. Harvest can take place as early as very late October and continue until January in mild climates or until frost arrives in colder places. Most growers pick the fruit, but it can be allowed to drop without damage since they remain hard as long as they are on the vine.

Cold storage prolongs the availability at the market so you can still find them in early spring.

Storing and Ripening
Kiwi store very nicely for several months if kept in a bag in your refrigerator. They can be stored for a short time at room temperature in an open bag away from other fruit.

When you are ready to soften the fruit for eating, remove desired quantity from storage bag and place in a plastic bag along with some fully ripe kiwi or other fully ripe fruit such as banana or apple. This ripe fruit gives off ethylene gas which hastens the ripening of any fruit near it. Keep the bag closed and the kiwi will be soft in about two to four days, depending on the length of time it has been stored and its maturity at time of harvest. The longer stored or the more mature it is, the faster it will soften.

Using

Most people peel the brown furry skin off the kiwi but you can eat the skin if you want after rubbing the fur off. (Do this while the kiwi is still hard.) An easy way to eat the whole fruit is to cut it in half either direction and scoop the fruit out with a spoon.

For use in fruit salads and desserts, you will probably want to peel the fruit first.

Remember to let the fruit harvested before full maturity ripen (get soft) before eating. Mature fruit can be eaten hard.

LOQUATS

Loquats are a yellow-orange to orange fruit resembling, at first glance, an apricot. They are a firmer and smoother-skinned fruit than the apricot and are much less fragile. They are quite juicy with a delightful, fairly mild flavor. They contain from 1 to 5 dark seeds which should be discarded.

This fruit, a favorite among Asians, is now gaining popularity with the rest of us. They are one of the delightful finds at our farmers' markets which have been important in bringing unusual fruits and vegetables to our attention. Those, like the loquat, which don't lend themselves well to mass handling and delays, usually aren't carried in the supermarket but can be brought to our markets easily.

Selecting
The different varieties vary in shape from somewhat elongated to rounded slightly tear drop-shaped, and in color from pale yellow-orange to rich orange. Color is the way to judge this fruit, the richest color for any given variety indicating the ripest and sweetest fruit.

The fruit should be firm without any wizening at the stem end which indicates that it is starting to dry out and is losing flavor. Scratches and scrapes on the skin do not detract from the eating quality.

They come to market either in bunches as they grow on the tree or as individual fruit cut from the bunches. Either way is fine. If you buy bunches and pay by the pound, remember that you are paying for the weight of the stems as well. The fruit in a bunch may not all ripen at the same time so be alert to underripe fruit.

Using
Loquats are ready to eat when you buy them. Asians peel this fruit, easily done by cutting or breaking off the stem end and then simply grasping the peel between thumb and finger and pulling downward. I, myself, eat them like an apricot or apple, discarding the blossom end and seeds but leaving the skin on.

Besides eating this fruit out of hand, try cutting them in half, removing the seeds and blossom end, and putting them in fruit salad. The cut surface does have a tendency to brown in the air. To prevent this as you prepare them, drop them into a bowl of lemon juice diluted with water, or into pineapple juice. Then remove and put into your salad.

Storage
Loquats keep nicely on the countertop for about a week.

Season
Late spring and early summer.

NOTES

MELONS

Three melon growers, Barbie Graper of Goleta, Pearl and Ed Munak of Paso Robles, and Sandy and Roger Sanders of Bakersfield have all contributed not only information but also many melons for the writing of this chapter. Consequently, I have been able to do extensive first-hand research and taste testing. I think I can safely say that the following information is reliable!

MUSKMELON/CANTALOUPE

There is a great deal of confusion regarding the names "muskmelon" and "cantaloupe".

Muskmelon is the heavily netted melon which has been grown in the United States for years, and which derives its name from its musky smell. It drops from the vine when ripe, leaving no trace of the stem on the fruit. Most growers harvest this melon with a gentle pull just before it is mature enough to drop. The flavor is at its best at that time.

The true cantaloupe comes from Cantalupo, Italy and new varieties such as Charentais and Vedrantais are now coming from France. They have varying degrees of netting. True cantaloupe never drop from the vine like muskmelon and the stems must be cut.

Cantaloupe and muskmelon are related and cross readily with one another.

The two most common questions that growers get asked about this fruit: "Is this ripe?" and "Is this ready to eat?" Maturity is achieved during growth on the vine and once the melon is harvested, no further improvement takes place. This means that the flavor will not improve by letting the melon sit around. It will soften, however, because of the ethylene gas given off by the seeds.

If the melon was picked at the proper time, you can eat it on the spot. It needs no further ripening (softening). If it was picked prematurely, it will be hard and benefit from waiting a few days for softening to take place.

Selecting muskmelon

How can you tell, then, which one has been picked at its prime as opposed to one that has been picked too soon? There are several things to check.

1. Smell, do not press, the stem end. (Pressing only causes damage.) It should smell so good that you want to eat it right then and there. (A ripe melon that has been refrigerated for an extensive time will lose this smell.)

2. Look at the stem end. A ripe melon is ready to fall off the vine so the break should be clean and smooth. If there is any stem at all remaining on the melon, it has been picked too soon.

3. Netting: most varieties raised in California are of the netted variety, that is, the skin has a raised netted appearance. Look for this netting. It should be over the whole melon, even on the spot where it has rested on the ground though perhaps less pronounced there. If netting is not good or missing altogether on patches of the melon, the flavor will be inferior.

4. Color: this is perhaps a less useful way to select a muskmelon as different varieties vary as to green or yellowish shadings. However, if there is a large container of melons, all the same variety, then select one that is the most yellow or the lightest green in its background color (the surface under the netting).

5. If there is a crack on the blossom end of the melon, smell for fermentation and look for mold on the surface. If neither of these is present and the melon meets all the other criteria, it will be good. But eat it promptly.

6. Shaking the melon is not a reliable test of ripeness since seeds do not always detach at maturity.

Selecting cantaloupe
Everything true for the muskmelon holds true for the cantaloupe except that there will be a piece of stem attached to the fruit.

Varieties
There are numerous varieties which may be round, oval, or fairly elongated. The flesh is usually orange but there are new green- fleshed hybrids. Some of the names you will hear are "Ambrosia", "Saticoy", and "Hales Best" in the muskmelon category and "Charentais" in the cantaloupe category.

Ambrosia cantaloupe

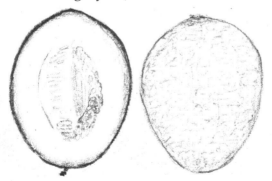

Saticoy cantaloupe

The Israeli Ha'ogen is a netted variety which drops off the vine leaving no stem but the netting is sparse and not a factor in judging quality. Use smell, stem end and color as your guides here.

Try different kinds to find the ones you prefer and to have the adventure of variety.

Season
Summer into fall. They can be grown throughout the state.

LATE MELONS

This group includes varieties of melons such as Casaba, Crenshaw, and Honeydew and are called late melons because they need a long, hot growing season. The melons in this group do not have the netting which distinguishes the muskmelon. They are a little more difficult to select than muskmelon and the main criterion is color.

Casaba - Choose deep orangey-yellow fruit. Paler yellow is less ripe.

Crenshaw - Depending on the variety, the color should be as yellow or orangey-yellow as possible though there will be a little green splashed here and there.

Honeydew - The color should be pale yellow with no hint of green and the surface will have a velvety finish.

Casaba

Boule d'Or - "Golden Ball", a large melon of French origin which gets its name from its round shape and gold color. The flesh is green and the rind hard.

Valencia - A Spanish melon with hard green rind and white to creamy flesh. It is shaped like a large acorn squash.

Other varieties - Choose by color and smelling the blossom end.

In these melons, a bright yellow patch on the surface of the skin is sunburn and does not affect the quality.

Season
Late summer into fall. They are grown in the hotter inland regions of the state.

WATERMELON

Selecting
It is perhaps best to rely on the grower for the quality. The picker can judge the growth of the fruit in the whole patch and look for the drying and curling of the little leaf right next to the stem, the indicators of a ripe

Crenshaw

Watermelon

melon. Since that is left behind on the vine, the customer doesn't have that help in making a selection.

Look on the side of the melon which rested on the ground. The color should be creamy rather than white.

Pearl Munak offers a method for picking out a high quality melon. While holding the melon in one hand, slap it with three fingers from the other hand. It should reverberate like a drum with a bright sound. If the sound is dull, the melon is overripe.

Varieties

There are more and more varieties all the time. There are small ones and giant ones, round ones and oval ones, good old seedy varieties and new seedless ones, and pink fleshed, red fleshed, and yellow fleshed ones.

Hybrids are developed to meet different needs such as disease and insect resistance, ripe appearance in unripe fruit (see stone fruit), greater size, and elimination of seeds. Keep in mind that flavor and fruit quality are often sacrificed for these other hybridized traits.

I suggest trying different kinds to find the flavor and texture you like best.

Storing

Ripe melons should be refrigerated for best keeping. I highly recommend that muskmelon and cantaloupe be wrapped well since their aroma permeates other things in the refrigerator. But remember that the wrapping keeps the ethylene gas in the fruit so it won't last as long as it would unwrapped. The seedless watermelons are good keepers because they don't have a mass of seeds giving off ethylene gas.

After cutting, melon must be refrigerated. Muskmelon and cantaloupe have a relatively short life span after cutting but late melons and watermelon are more durable. Cover cut surfaces with plastic wrap.

RECIPES

In the process of testing so many melons, I had to do something more than eat them all fresh and plain. How can only two people eat a whole giant Crenshaw melon? Following are some recipes I developed.

Crenshaw Melon Pickles

5 lbs. prepared melon (approx. 12 cups)

6 c water

6 T salt

3 c water

3 1/2 c apple cider vinegar

6 c sugar

3 sticks cinnamon

3 T whole cloves

1 orange, seeds removed, thinly sliced and quartered

1 lemon, seeds removed, thinly sliced and quartered

Remove the heart of the melon for eating fresh, leaving about one inch of melon on the outer edge. Peel skin off and cut into bite size pieces. Place in glass, ceramic or stainless container, cover with brine of water and salt.

Let stand 12 to 24 hours at room temperature.

Pour off brine and let drain in colander.

Into large stainless steel cookpot, measure water, vinegar, sugar, cinnamon and cloves. Boil approximately 1/2 hour until somewhat thickened. Add orange and lemon, boil 2 minutes longer.

Add melon rind and simmer 5 minutes. Then bring to rapid boil for one minute, fill sterilized jars and seal at once.

Let stand two weeks before serving.

Yield: 6 pints

Casaba Melon Shake

1 c small melon pieces

2 T lemon juice

1/2 c frozen vanilla yogurt

Whirl melon in blender until it becomes pureed, add lemon juice and yogurt. Blend. Drink immediately.

Yield: 1 serving

NOTES

PASSION FRUIT

The name of this fruit comes from its intricate flower which appears to Christians to have symbols of the Crucifixion. The flavor of this fruit is so delightful that it is possible for one also to develop a "passion" for eating it.

Passion fruit are almost round fruit, just a little longer than they are wide. The ones grown here in California are the purple variety and range in size from a large walnut to well over 2" from end to end. Inside the leathery skin there is a mass of tiny, black, tear drop-shaped seeds, each encased in its own bright yellow pulp.

Selecting
They are usually smooth when harvested but aren't ready to eat until the skin has dried and shriveled and started turning brown. You can buy them smooth and purple, or rumply and partly brown to all brown, depending upon how soon you want to eat them. They should be free of cracks but funny tan and whitish spots make no difference.

If there is a difference in weight between fruit of the same size and degree of ripeness, choose the heavier as it will have more juice.

Size is a matter of personal preference, though if the fruit is being sold by the piece, you will get more for your money by selecting the larger pieces.

Using
When the skin is still smooth and purple the fruit is tart and less juicy. The crinklier and browner the skin turns, the sweeter and juicier the pulp becomes.

To eat fresh, cut the fruit in half and scoop the pulp out with a spoon. Eat seeds and all. Or cut just the end off and squeeze the pulp into your mouth.

The seedy pulp makes an excellent topping for vanilla ice cream or plain or vanilla yogurt.

You can make a seedless puree by sieving the pulp. The puree can be used in meat marinades, as a sauce over ice cream or yogurt, or mixed with fruit and fruit juices.

Ripening and Storing
If you buy the fruit still smooth and purple, leave it on your counter out of the sun to dry and ripen. It will take about five to seven days before it is ready to eat, longer if the fruit is very firm when you buy it. If you buy the fruit completely wrinkled and brown, you can eat it right away. In between these extremes the ripening time will vary.

Ripe fruit can be stored in the refrigerator several days or it can be frozen. You can freeze the fruit whole, or as puree either with or without the seeds.

Season
August into October.

NOTES

PEARS

There are two basic kinds of pears, European and Asian. The European pear is the familiar fruit with the typical pear shape and is eaten soft. The Asian pear is a relative newcomer to California, has a rounder shape and is eaten crunchy.

EUROPEAN PEARS

The Delta area south of Sacramento is a major pear growing region in our state. Primarily Bartlett is grown here. An interesting drive takes one south along the levee road beside the Sacramento River where pear orchards stretch, one after the other, as far as the eye can see.

Bill and Barbara Carr have been raising pears in this region for twenty seven years. Barbara was a school teacher and Bill was an editor at the Sacramento Bee until their retirement a few years ago. But they didn't retire from their pear business which is thriving and reaches its peak in midsummer.

I had a delightful visit with them just before harvesting began. They answered all my questions and gave me a tour of their orchard as well.

European pears are one of our fruits which need to be picked "green" or hard. If they are allowed to ripen fully on the tree, they lose flavor, the texture becomes mealy and the center at the core is likely to turn brown.

Maturity and readiness to pick are judged by sugar content. As sugar develops, the pressure inside the pear drops. This pressure can be measured, enabling the grower to pick his crop at the optimum time for the finest quality. There is no way to tell by looking at the fruit if it has reached that optimum quality so you must rely on the grower.

Selecting

The pears at the market may be newly picked and unripe or they may be partially or fully ripe. The hard pears will be the most durable for transporting in your basket. Treat ready-to-eat fruit very gently as it is fragile.

Many pears have a pink blush on one side. This coloring is caused by the sun but does not affect the quality of the fruit, either for better or for worse. It looks lovely, though.

Sunburn, which does have a negative effect on quality, shows up as a dark spot with a whitish ring around it. Fruit with sunburn would be considered second quality and should sell at a reduced price.

Fruit handled carefully will not have blemishes, which show up as brown streaks or spots. However, as long as such blemishes are only skin deep, eating quality will still be excellent.

Avoid fruit with bruised spots unless it is sold at a lower price and you don't mind cutting out the damaged areas. Such fruit will need to be used promptly but may be just what you want. You can probably get good halves from such fruit for canning and the rest will make excellent jam or butter, fresh pear sauce, or dice up nicely for fruit salad.

Since size has no bearing on fruit quality, select according to your purposes. Smaller ones will be more efficient for canning, larger ones easier for jam, and whatever size fits your appetite for eating fresh!

Ripening

Put hard pears in a dark cool place. For small quantities, a brown paper bag on your kitchen counter is ideal. For larger quantities, try a wine cellar or a shallow carton covered with newspaper. If the pears were just picked, they will need up to two weeks to become ready to eat. Later in the season, they may ripen in as little time as four to five days. Peek in your dark closet or covered container periodically to check on progress and remove the fruit as it ripens.

The easiest and best way to judge when a Bartlett pear is ready to eat is by color. There is no need at all to use a touch test and risk bruising. When it is yellow, it is ready. For canning purposes, the fruit should still be firm and just barely yellow.

Russeted pears like Bosc and Comice and the new red Bartlett pear develop color before the pear is ripe so you will need to apply very gentle pressure to the stem end to feel softness or hold the fruit in the palm of your hand and feel the whole for a sense of softness just as you do for avocados. In either case, handle the fruit very gently.

Storage

If you want to hold the fruit for an extended time, place it in your refrigerator while it is still green or hard. It will actually ripen in the chill but at a greatly reduced speed. Remove fruit as you want it and ripen as described above. If you see pears starting to ripen in this cold storage, it is best not to try to hold them. Take them out, finish the ripening, and plan to use them soon.

Once the fruit is ready to eat, it will hold in your refrigerator only a very few days.

Season

Bartlett pears are one of the earliest varieties, starting in mid-July and continuing into August. Other varieties range from late summer into the fall. The location of the orchard will be a factor as is true with other fruits. If the grower is large-scale, he may be able to extend his season with cold storage. Don't hesitate to check with the grower if you want to know how long ago the fruit was picked.

RECIPES

Barbara Carr says that her customers wonder what they can do with pears besides eat them fresh. She tells them to use them the same ways they use apples. Throughout the many years that she has been selling pears, she has handed out recipes to her customers and the following are the ones most asked for.

Pear Nut Bread

2-3 ripe pears	2 c sifted flour
1 c sugar	1/4 t cinnamon
1/2 c salad oil	1/4 t nutmeg
2 eggs	1 t soda
1 t vanilla	1/2 t salt
1/4 c sour cream	3/4 c chopped nuts

Peel and core pears, chop to get 1 cup. In large bowl, beat together oil and sugar until well blended. Beat in eggs, one at a time, sour cream, and vanilla. Sift together dry ingredients. Add to wet mixture; blend well. Add pears and nuts. Put batter in greased and floured loaf pan. Bake at 350° one hour, or until toothpick inserted in center comes out clean. Cool in pan 10 min. Turn onto rack to finish cooling. Makes 1 large or 2 medium (2 1/2x7 1/2) loaves.

Gourmet Pear Pie

Pastry for a 10", one-crust pie

Flour	Margarine
About 8 ripe pears	Cinnamon
Lemon juice	Nutmeg

Line a 10" deep pie pan with pastry. Dust with flour. Peel, core, and slice pears into shell. Sprinkle with lemon juice, cinnamon, and nutmeg. Dot with margarine. Cover with batter mix.

Batter

1/4 lb margarine	2 T flour
1 c sugar	1 t vanilla
2 eggs	

Cream margarine and sugar. Add eggs and flour and beat until creamy. Add vanilla and blend. Pour over pears. Bake at 350° one hour to 1 hour, 10 min.

This pie freezes well. Thaw in slow oven (225°) about 2 hours.

NOTE: I made this pie, omitting the crust since I wanted to avoid the calories, cholesterol, and I admit, the work! It was still excellent, hot from the oven through the time it was thoroughly cooled. (I ate small servings every twenty minutes or so. After all, I felt obligated to test it thoroughly for the purpose of this book and I can report that it is outstanding at all temperatures!)

Pear Breakfast Cookies

1 1/2 c diced fresh pears (2 pears)

1/2 c margarine	1 t baking powder
1/3 c honey	1/2 t salt
1/2 c brown sugar	1 c rolled oats
1 egg	1/3 c raisins
1 t vanilla	1/3 c chopped nuts
1 c sifted flour	

Cream margarine, honey, and sugar. Add egg, beating until light and fluffy. Add vanilla. Sift together flour, baking powder and salt. Add to creamed mix. Stir in oats, pears, raisins, and nuts. Drop by teaspoonfuls on lightly greased baking sheet. Bake at 400° 10-12 min. Makes 4 dozen.

Cranberry Baked Pears

6 large ripe pears	1/8 t cardamom
2 1/2 c cranberry juice	12 whole cloves
1/2 c honey	2 small cinnamon sticks
1/4 t red food coloring	

Preheat oven to 350°. In 3 qt. casserole mix juice, honey, coloring, and cardamom. Peel pears, leaving stems intact. Cut thin slice from bottom so pears stand upright when served. Place pears on side in juice mix. Add cloves and cinnamon. Bake 50 min. occasionally turning and basting pears. Refrigerate several hours, turning and basting for even color. Arrange upright in serving dish; strain extra juice over. These freeze well. Delicious partially thawed.

Green Pear Preserves

1 part sugar to 2 parts green pears, peeled and cut into small pieces. Lemon juice, about 2 t per 1 lb. pears.

Mix all and let refrigerate overnight. Next day bring to fast boil. Lower heat and simmer gently until mixture is golden, fruit is transparent and mixture reaches desired consistency. Seal at once in hot sterilized jars.

Pear Butter

Wash pears; slice without removing peels or cores; place in a heavy kettle with just enough water to cover bottom. Cook until very soft; force through sieve to remove skins and seeds. Measure and add half as much sugar as pulp. Add spices if desired.

Cook, stirring frequently, until smooth and thick enough to spread. Pour immediately into hot sterilized jars and seal at once.

This next recipe is one Barbara hands out along with the ones above. It comes from her sister-in-law, Pauline Spirz, of Santa Barbara. Pauline entered this mincemeat in the Cortland Pear Fair and won a blue ribbon with it.

Pear Mincemeat

15 lbs. fresh ripe pears	2 t cinnamon
3 c unsweetened pineapple juice	1 t allspice
3 c brown sugar, packed	1 t nutmeg
2 c snipped, pitted prunes	1 t salt
2 c seedless raisins	

Pare, core, and coarsely dice pears to get 6 qts. Turn into large, heavy kettle with pineapple juice. Add remaining ingredients and bring to boil, stirring occasionally until sugar dissolves. Boil slowly about 1 1/2 hours, stirring occasionally to prevent sticking, until mixture is slightly thickened. Spoon into hot jars, seal and process in hot water bath 20 min. Makes 4 quarts.

ASIAN PEARS

These pears are also commonly called apple pears because of their resemblance to apples in shape and crispness. However, they are true pears which come from Japan and China and have the texture and wonderfully juicy quality of pears. They have a milder flavor than the European pear.

While a few varieties resemble the European pear in shape, most are quite round and even flattened. They range in size from quite small to very large. Color depends upon variety and ranges from green to yellow-green to russet.

Selecting
These pears should ripen on the tree, unlike their European cousins. Since they stay firm, color is the key to selecting them. You will need to rely on the grower to let you know the ripe color of the variety or varieties he raises. Then be sure to get the richest colored of the variety.

Here are a few of the varieties and their colors:

Tsu Li - green

Ya Li - light yellow-green

Shinseiki - yellow

Chojuro - russet

Try different varieties to find your favorites since the flavors vary from one kind to another.

Using

Because these pears are so crisp, they hold their shape beautifully and make a nice addition to fruit salads. They also travel well in a picnic basket or lunch box without bruising like the European pear.

They are most often eaten fresh but can be cooked. They require a longer cooking time than European pears and retain their shape much like quince. (Quince and pears are related to one another as members of the apple family.)

Season

Summer through fall.

Storage

These pears will keep on your counter up to two weeks and for several months in your refrigerator.

PEPINO

Although this fruit has been cultivated for a long time, it has only recently been gaining popularity in the United States. A few California growers are starting to raise pepino on a commercial basis.

Pepinos are a subtropical fruit which grow on perennial bushes related to eggplant and potato. They are often called pepino melons. They are shaped much like a tear drop, broad at the stem end and tapering to a point at the blossom end. Size ranges from very small to very large. The skin is thin, very smooth and shiny. They have an orangey-yellow background color with purple stripes.

Selecting

Color is the most important factor in making your selection. The background color should be turning yellow to orange-yellow. If it is, the fruit is mature and will complete its ripening. If the background color is still green, you will take a chance that the fruit was picked before it reached great enough maturity to ripen. If it was picked too soon, the fruit will wrinkle and never be edible. If you find you must purchase the fruit green, be sure to look for the lightest green possible.

Pepino

Size is irrelevant except as it pertains to your use. You might want small ones for little snacks and large ones for a showy dessert.

Ripening

Pepinos should be allowed to reach their full orange-yellow background color before they are eaten. Just let them sit on your counter or in a fruit bowl. They will ripen faster if they are in proximity to other ripe fruit such as bananas. They are eaten firm, though they can be slightly soft. If they are allowed to get very soft, they are overripe and lose their delicious flavor.

Using

Pepinos are almost always eaten fresh. If you like the skin, you can eat the fruit whole. If you prefer not to eat the skin, cut the fruit in half lengthwise and scoop out the flesh.

Storing

Pepinos can be left on your kitchen counter until soft, the length of time depending upon the maturity of the fruit and the length of time since harvest. Once soft and ready to eat, it can be stored for a few days in your refrigerator.

RECIPES

Pepino Tapioca

1 1/2 c apple/pear juice

2 T sugar

2 T + 1 t tapioca

1 1/2 c diced pepino, seeds removed

Mix juice, sugar, and tapioca in saucepan. Let stand 5 minutes. Bring to boil and cook two minutes. Add diced pepino. Pour into serving dish or into individual serving dishes.

Cold Fruit Soup

1 cup mashed strawberries (approx. 1/2 pound)

3/4 c mashed pepino (2 medium large pepinos)

1 medium size sweet eating apple, diced

2 T sugar if desired

Mix all ingredients together and serve chilled.

Hot Fruit Soup

Follow recipe above except substitute a tart apple for the sweet apple. Place all ingredients in saucepan, heat but do not boil. Serve steaming hot.

PERSIMMONS

With their smooth skin and bright orange color, persimmons, I think, are one of the most beautiful fruits we have . They are magnificent in a fruit display, both at the farmer's stand and in one's own kitchen.

There are two species of persimmon, American and Oriental. The American persimmon is native to parts of the eastern United States and bears small fruit, all astringent when hard. You are unlikely to find any out here in California. The persimmons at our California markets are Oriental varieties, much larger than the American. Most are astringent but there are nonastringent varieties as well. By far, the most common varieties at our markets are the Hachiya and Fuju.

HACHIYA

Selecting

Hachiya persimmons are the large elongated fruit usually found in commercial markets. They are a variety which is astringent until very soft. These fruit can be allowed to ripen on the tree but since they are very fragile when ripe (and since the birds have a passion for the ripe fruit) they are almost always picked while they are still hard. The grower judges when to pick by the color.

Hachiya
Persimmon

The fruit start out green and gradually turn to a deep orange while still hard. Once picked, they continue to develop deeper color, changing to a red orange as they become soft. You will want to avoid fruit which have green tints as they were picked early and will be less flavorful and sweet although they will ripen and be usable.

You can purchase hard fruit for later use or ripe fruit for use immediately or in a few days. Fruit ready to eat is always at a premium so you might want to plan ahead, getting a few hard fruit each week and doing your own ripening.

Try to purchase fruit which has been handled very carefully. My experience in raising and selling them indicates that fruit allowed to remain on the tree until maximum maturity before softening is most fragile. It is picked still firm but it is no longer very hard. These fruit must be handled individually and preferably not piled because they bruise when piled and poured. The bruises don't show up until later.

115

Large-scale growers with hundreds of trees and many employees usually harvest their persimmons earlier than maximum maturity and bring them to market heaped in boxes. It is not cost effective for them to wait for maximum maturity, pick them one at a time as I do and place them in single layers. They will also be less expensive than mine.

That is one of the nice things about a farmers' market. You have choices not offered in a grocery store.

Sometimes persimmons will have very dark, almost black areas on the skin. This has no effect on the quality.

Ripening

Simply leave the fruit on your counter out of the sun or place it in a paper bag the way you do avocados. The length of time it takes to ripen will depend on how mature the fruit was when it was picked, and the temperature in your room. Remember that these persimmons must be **very** soft before eating and it may take more than a week. They will become almost translucent, rich orange red in color and almost like gelatin in feel.

If you notice bad spots developing as the fruit softens, you can do one of several things.

> If you have your heart set on a soft persimmon to eat fresh, let it continue to ripen but realize that the spoilage will spread and you will lose a substantial portion of the fruit.

> Remove the spoiled area immediately and dry the fruit (see below) while still firm.

> Remove the spoiled area and freeze. If the persimmon is close to getting soft, freezing removes the astringency. You can then eat it partially thawed as a fruit slush or completely thawed. If the fruit is still quite hard, freezing will remove only part of the astringency.

Eating

The fruit may be eaten whole, skin and all though some people discard the skin. Eat it out of hand or use a spoon.

If you freeze individual ripe fruit, you can remove them from the freezer a short time before serving to partially thaw. They make a delicious fruit ice just as is with no work or added calories.

Drying

You can also dry these persimmons. During our first fall season out here in California, we visited my brother, David Luce, and his wife Nina. They have a Hachiya tree and Nina had whole persimmons hanging by string to dry in front of a large window. They looked absolutely beautiful.

116

I decided to dry some of ours so Nina explained to me that they needed to be peeled first and then hung by the stem. Home I went and picked some fruit. As they ripened, (I knew these persimmons had to be very soft before eating) I struggled to peel and then hang them. I put them at the west facing picture window in our living room right above the sofa. As the days passed, I noticed some were showing signs of sweat and mold. Then they began dripping. Then they began dropping off their strings and going splat on the back of the sofa!

I have to tell you, the poor sofa was never the same after that and I have never lived it down with my family.

Here's the right way to dry whole persimmons. Do not wait for them to get ripe. Peel them while they are still firm, leaving the stem on. Then tie a string onto the stem and hang in a southern exposure where they get as much sun as possible. They will shrink considerably and are ready when they are pliable but not sticky.

You may also peel and slice the fruit to dry in bite size pieces.

FUJU

Selecting
These are a flatter persimmon that are usually eaten hard like an apple. Again, the grower uses color as his guide to picking. They start out green and gradually turn deeper and deeper orange just as do the Hachiya. Just as with them, you will want to avoid the fruit with a greenish cast as it has not matured enough on the tree and will lack flavor and sweetness.

Fuju persimmon

These fruit are much sturdier than the Hachiya and can be handled carefully in quantity without bruising. Since Fuju are edible from the moment of picking, selecting is simple. They should have good color and be as blemish-free as possible.

As with Hachiya, Fuju sometimes have a very dark area on the skin and again, it has no detrimental effect on the quality.

Eating
Not only can you eat these persimmons hard, but you can let them get moderately soft and eat them that way. That means they have good storing qualities. You can buy a quantity at the end of the season to eat over many weeks.

These persimmons dry just as nicely as the hachiya. If you have a dehydrator, you might want to try drying a large quantity to take you through the winter and spring.

Other varieties
There are a number of other varieties including Giant Fuju, Chocolate, and Tamopan. Check with the grower about the astringency of his particular varieties.

Season - late fall

NOTES

POMEGRANATE

These are showy bright red or pinkish-red fruit with an interesting blossom end that extends down about an inch, still holding the dried delicate stamens. The fruit are usually about 3 or 4 inches in diameter but can be smaller or larger depending on variety, climate, etc. They are roundish but if you look, you will see that they are actually five sided fruit.

Most are grown in the warmer inland areas of the state but they can be grown along the coast where they will be slightly less sweet.

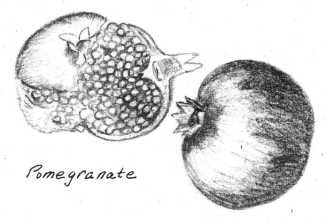

Pomegranate

Season
Pomegranates first appear in our markets in mid-September and can be found through December.

Selecting
Color is a primary trait to look for. Pomegranates develop their sugar content as they mature and gain color. However, as they reach full maturity and turn deep red, they develop a higher acid content which means that they become more tart.

For eating fresh, you may want to select lighter pinkish-red fruit. For making jelly, you should choose the deep purple-red.

Weight is another test of quality. The heavier the fruit is for its size, the more seeds and juice it will contain.

Softness - Pomegranates are ready to eat when you buy them whether they are firm or soft. They start out firm and become softer as they sit.

Using
The fruit is ready to eat when you buy it. You can store it at room temperature for some days and up to two or three months in a cool dry place.

The interior of the fruit has pockets of moist red seeds separated by white membrane. Use only the seed portion, discarding the membrane and outer skin. You can eat the seeds just as they are or you can juice the fruit.

To remove seeds:
The first time I ate a pomegranate, I cut it open with a knife and used a spoon to

scoop out the seeds. By the time I was done, the sink, the plants on the windowsill and I were all covered with bright red spots. So the second time, I put on a bib apron and went outdoors where I didn't have to worry about juice spritzing all over. The third time, I figured there had to be a better way.

The juice of the pomegranate is contained in the bright red nodules surrounding the seeds and as you scoop, you break some of these nodules open. As they break, they burst, sending forth a shower of juice. The secret then is to remove the seeds without breaking any of the nodules.

Either score the skin to get a start on removing it or make one bold cut to halve the fruit. Once you have access to the inside, peel the skin back a little at a time to free sections of membrane. Then pull the membrane away from the seeds. With this technique you seldom break a nodule and the job goes very quickly.

You can eat the seeds as you remove them or you can save them to use in fruit salad or as a garnish on meat dishes or desserts. They freeze nicely for later use as a garnish or addition to a fruit salad.

Juicing:
For a single serving of juice, roll the fruit on a hard surface to bruise it thoroughly, puncture a hole for a straw, and enjoy the juice this way.

For larger quantities of juice, use a juicer which will separate the membrane out for you. There are many elaborate juicers on the market now and you can ask about their capabilities in regard to pomegranate juicing. An old-fashioned hand squeezer works moderately well and you can use a strainer or sieve to remove the pieces of membrane that break off into the juice.

PRICKLY PEAR

I have discovered some interesting things about the prickly pear, thanks to Joan and Bart LaGreca of Santa Barbara. They have sold at our market for a number of years, specializing in beautiful bouquets of flowers. But they also have some wonderful fruits, including the prickly pear.

Bart, now retired, spent many years working for the Blood Bank. He was head of the lab at Tri-Counties Blood Bank for ten years and then became Managing Director for twenty years. He was also an inspector for the American Assoc. of Blood Banks for ten years and served several terms on the Board of Directors for the State Blood Bank Systems.

Joan graduated from the Royal College of Art in London as a watercolorist and painted sets for ballet productions at the Lobero Theater in Santa Barbara during the late sixties and early seventies. She also had her own florist shop for eleven years.

December at the Santa Barbara Farmers' Market brings out the creative side of some of our growers. For the first three Saturdays of the month growers and their families who are handcrafters and artists can sell their work alongside their fruits, vegetables and flowers. Joan brings a touch of class to this event with her framed watercolors and beautiful holiday centerpieces of greens and flowers and ribbons.

A Little Bit of History

Joan LaGreca has done research on prickly pears and shared some interesting information with me. They are grown in the drier southwestern portion of the United States and in Mexico, also in areas with more moderate rainfall such as Florida, Brazil and northern Argentina.

They have even been introduced into Mediterranean countries, India, Ceylon, South Africa, the Canary Islands, and Madagascar. There seem to be two chief reasons for their wide spread: their food value and their use in the cochineal dye industry. The cochineal insect which gives a red dye feeds on the prickly pear.

Another interesting piece of information Joan shared with me concerns their use in Italy. They are often planted in the lava seams of Mount Vesuvius where their roots readily grow into the cracks in the rock, eventually making the barren earth suitable for other plants.

Bart and Joan gave me the opportunity to go out to their place and do some picking firsthand. I wore heavy denim pants, long sleeves, and a pair of yellow rubber gloves such as one uses to scrub the floor or do other household chores. I managed to get one thorn from the plant itself into my leg through the denim and a few of the fine thorns in my arms but they turned out to be almost no problem at all. The fine ones washed out and the other one got along painlessly with my body until it finally worked its way out!

Bart helped me pick a fairly large quantity which I took home in brown paper bags.

This fruit is often sold with the thorns intact which to me has been a deterrent to the purchasing of it. Books I have read talk about using tongs while scalding and peeling which also has been a deterrent to me. But Bart always removes the thorns from his fruit before selling it and his remarkably simple solution to all these "thorny" problems is that pair of yellow rubber household gloves.

After I got home I put my gloves back on and rubbed over the entire surface of each fruit to remove the thorns, letting the thorns fall into a brown paper bag. Then, with the gloves still on, I washed the pears thoroughly under running water to make sure all the thorns were gone. This approach is quick, easy, and safe, and the subsequent work with the pears is just as easy as it is with peaches or tomatoes.

Prickly pear

Season late summer and fall

Selecting
Prickly pears come in red, orange, and white varieties, the white being less common. The size varies from approximately 2 1/4" long to 4 or 4 1/2" long with the diameter proportionate to the length. The size and color don't make any difference in quality.

Storing
Prickly pears can be kept at room temperature approximately 4 or 5 days. After that time, they begin to crinkle though they can still be eaten. In the refrigerator they will keep a month or more. Spoilage is easily detected as brown mushy spots. Any bad spots should be removed.

Using
Remove thorns as described above.

Eating fresh
The common way to eat this fruit fresh out of hand is to simply break or cut it in half and eat the seedy pulp which makes up the biggest part of the fruit. The seeds are extremely hard so don't bite down on them, just swallow. It is a bit difficult, but try eating the fleshy layer just under the paper thin skin rather than throwing it away.

Preparing puree and seeded pear pieces

To peel, scald the fruit just as you do tomatoes or peaches. The very thin skin will peel off in the same way as it does for those other fruits.

Next, cut the fruit in quarters lengthwise. Scoop out the seedy pulp and place in one container. Place the pear pieces in another container. Be sure to get all the seeds removed from the pear pieces since biting down unexpectedly on even one seed of such a hard variety can be unpleasant and even painful.

Sieve the seedy pulp with a wooden spoon and wire sieve. This is a very quick and easy way to get rid of the seeds without losing all that juicy pulp.

Now that you have seeded pear pieces and seedless puree, you are ready for all kinds of recipes.

Freezing

You can freeze prepared puree and pieces. It is ideal to have this preparation done before freezing but if you are too busy at the time of harvest to do the preparation, simply freeze whole prickly pears (thorns removed) for use at a later time. After removing them from the freezer, let them thaw a short time, then remove the skin just as you do after scalding. If you let them thaw too much, it will be somewhat more difficult to get the skin off. Continue preparing as for fresh pears.

RECIPES

Prickly Pear Gelatin

Important note: Prickly pear must be cooked in order to jell. After several tries at making gelatin, varying proportions each time, and having no success at all, it occurred to me that prickly pear might be like pineapple. One more experiment proved this to be the case.

1 c prickly pear puree

1 c water

2 T lime juice

1/4 c sugar

1 pkg. gelatin

Boil water and puree together for 2 minutes. Add lime juice. Mix gelatin and sugar together, add to puree and stir until gelatin is completely dissolved. Chill until set.

Prickly Pear Yogurt

Stir prickly pear puree into nonfat plain yogurt. Add pieces as well if you have extra.

Prickly Pear Peach Tapioca Pudding

1 c prickly pear puree

1/2 c peach juice or liquid from frozen peaches, thawed

1/2 c prickly pear pieces

2/3 c peach pieces

2 T sugar

2 T plus 1 t tapioca

Mix puree, juice, sugar and tapioca. Let stand 5 minutes. Bring to boil and cook 2 minutes, add fruit and boil 1/2 minute more. Pour into serving bowl or individual serving dishes.

Prickly Pear Cake

1/2 c shortening	2 1/4 c flour
1 1/4 c sugar	1 t soda
2 eggs, slightly beaten	1 t cinnamon
1 1/4 c prickly pear puree	1 c raisins
1 c prickly pear pieces	

Cream shortening and sugar, add eggs and mix well. Sift dry ingredients together. Add alternately with puree. Stir in prickly pear pieces and raisins last. Bake in 9" square pan at 350° for approx. 1 hour.

Dried Prickly Pear Pieces

Follow directions with dehydrator. They take only about 6 to 8 hours to dry into a very high quality colorful fruit.

QUINCE

Quince was a common fruit years ago when homemakers put up pickles and preserves as a part of everyday life. Because canning is done far less now and because this fruit must be cooked before eating, it has become a specialty fruit.

I remember a quince bush at our farm when I was a child and I remember my mother making quince jelly. The

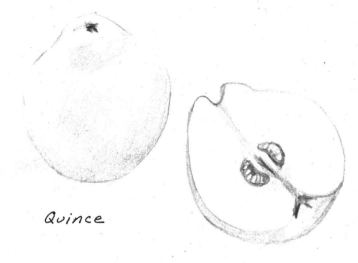

Quince

fruit was rather small, probably a very old variety, so it was a surprise to find such large quince at our California Farmers' Markets.

This fruit can be fairly round or pear shaped but will be somewhat irregular. It can have fuzzy or smooth skin and some varieties can reach 6" to 8" in diameter. Most of the ones you will find at the market will be more like 4" in diameter.

Selecting

Size - not a factor in selecting except as it pertains to your use.

Color - Mature fruit will be yellowish green or golden yellow. Do not get green fruit as it is not mature.

Aroma - Ripe fruit has a delightful aroma so smell is a good test of maturity.

Shape - not important except that for recipes requiring peeled fruit, a relatively smooth fruit is easier to prepare than a gnarly one.

Bruises - Although quince is a hard fruit, it bruises easily and should be handled carefully. Avoid fruit that is bruised unless you can get a good buy and use it promptly.

Using

Quince are used hard. They are not a sub-tropical fruit which need to sit on your counter to soften before using. They are always cooked. Leave the fuzz on the fruit (if it has fuzz) until you are ready to use it. Then rub it off easily.

Since quince hold their shape very nicely when cooked they can be used in many recipes. You will need to peel and core them first when baking them like apples, when using them in such recipes as baked chicken, or when making pickles.

For recipes which call for quince juice or sauce, you need only to wash and cut up the fruit before simmering in water for about 3/4 to 1 hour. The amount of fruit and water vary according to the recipe you are using and the intensity of flavor you desire.

For juice, put stewed quince in jelly bag to drain or pour into colander lined with about four layers of dampened cheesecloth.

For sauce or puree, put stewed fruit through a foodmill.

You might want to check through your grandmother's cookbooks or haunt second-hand bookstores for old cookbooks to discover interesting old recipes.

Storage
Quince will keep on your kitchen counter for about a week but much longer in your refrigerator. Keep an eye on them so you can use any that show signs of bruises and spoilage.

Season
Very late summer and fall.

RHUBARB

Rhubarb is an unusual "fruit" in that it is not a fruit at all but rather a stem which we prepare as a fruit.

Selecting

At our farmers' markets you can find individual stems with the leaves still attached and bundles of stems with the leaves removed. Either way is fine though you have a better idea of freshness if the leaves are still on. If the leaves are still attached, they should be very large and perky though the sun beating down on them at the market causes them to wilt. The leaves *must* be removed and discarded since they are poisonous. If the leaves have been removed, the leaf end should look freshly cut rather than very dried out.

Crispness: The stems should be crisp, not limp.

Color: Variety determines color which can be solid green, solid red, or red at the lower end turning to green at the upper end. Many people prefer the red for its lovely appearance but they are all equally good in terms of flavor. Since rhubarb stems are pulled, the bottom end will flare out into a lovely pastel shade.

Size: Some stems are long and slender, others shorter and very fat. Size has little bearing on quality.

Season

Rhubarb is available in the spring and into early summer back east but out here in California, it is available for a slightly longer time. Be cautious of rhubarb late in its season since the stems can become pithy.

Using

Rhubarb is always cooked and sweetened.

RECIPES

Rhubarb Sauce

Wash stems, cut into 1" lengths and simmer with the water that remains from the washing until tender. Add sugar to suit your taste and eat warm or cold.

My mother has passed on to me some fascinating old cookbooks, one of which is *The Chicago Record Cook Book* which belonged to my grandmother and was published in 1896. The title page has these words:

Seasonable, inexpensive bills of fare for
every day in the year,

Designed to furnish "good living," in appetizing variety,
at an expense not to exceed $500 a year

for a family of five; arranged so that remnants
from one day can frequently be used with menus of the next.

1,100 prize menus with recipes, carefully indexed, the
cream of 10,000 manuscripts contributed by the
women of America to the Chicago Record's
daily contest for menus for a day.

In this cookbook, rhubarb is called pieplant and the following two recipes come from this book.

Pieplant Meringue Pie - Either fresh or canned pieplant may be used for this. Take enough stewed pieplant for one pie - about half a pint - and stir into it while boiling a heaping teaspoonful of cornstarch mixed with the yolks of two eggs and a cup of sugar and one tablespoonful of butter; have ready a pie tin lined with a nice crust already baked. Spread this with the pieplant mixture and cover with a meringue made of the whites of the eggs, beaten stiff, with two tablespoonfuls of sugar. Set in the oven until nicely browned and serve cold. Delicious.

Harriet Mann.

No.1421 Central street, Evanston, Ill.

Pieplant Bird's Nest - Butter a pie-plate well, wash the pieplant, but do not peel; cut in very small pieces and fill the tin half full. Make a batter of one cup sour milk, one cup sour cream, one egg, one teaspoonful soda, pinch of salt and flour to make stiff batter; pour this over the pieplant. Bake one-half hour in a quick oven and eat with sweetened cream. This can be made of other kinds of fruit.

Shirley de Forest.

Box 596, Janesville, Wis.

It is interesting to note that oven temperatures were not used in recipes at this time. It is also interesting to note that "street" in the address is not capitalized.

SAPOTE

I visited B.D. Dautch at his farm in Carpinteria where he raises vegetables, herbs, and fruit. He was born in Buffalo, NY in 1950.

"I led a typically TV-laden, junk food oriented, athletic life 'til the age of 16 when nature and Existentialism became prominent influences along with beer, girls, etc. (this was the 60's)".

After graduating from the University of Pennsylvania with a degree in history, gardening came into his life, first in New Hampshire, then in California. After a sixteen month trip to India and Indonesia, he returned to California and a 23 acre certified organic farm. He now farms seven acres, four of which he owns, all in Carpinteria.

"I have *never* used chemical fertilizers or sprayed an herbicide or pesticide in my farming career," he says.

He and Liz live with their young son and baby daughter in a home designed and built by themselves with the help of friends.

B.D. was very generous with time and information for this book. Among other things, we talked about sapote.

Sapote are another of our subtropical fruits but the tree is hardier to California's semi-arid climate than many other subtropical fruits because of its tap root which reaches down to deeper water. Although it has been around for many years, it hasn't enjoyed a surge in popularity such as kiwi and cherimoya have recently had.

Don't deprive yourself of this delicious fruit just because it hasn't made the "top ten".

Selecting the fruit

There are white and black varieties but you will be likely to find only white varieties at the market. They are a somewhat round fruit with the blossom end dropping into a little point. They have very thin skin, pale green to greenish yellow in color, depending on variety.

Sapote

These fruit can ripen fully on the tree but you will almost surely not get a truly tree-ripened fruit at the market because of their fragility. The trees become very large and ripe fruit does not hold. When it falls it becomes hopelessly damaged for marketing purposes.

Therefore, growers harvest the fruit just before it gets soft. Color is their indication when to pick. They wait for the dark unripe green color to turn to the lighter green in the greener variety and to a yellowish green in the more yellow variety. Avoid fruit that is dark green, indicating that it was picked too soon. This fruit will wrinkle and not soften up properly.

B.D. tells me that the fruit on the sunnier side of the tree will be more yellow and sweeter than fruit from the northern side of the tree. Ideally he waits for as much yellow as possible before picking. The fruit does not change color once it is picked.

You will be able to purchase the fruit at this newly picked stage of firmness, or at any degree of softness up to the fruit that is ready to eat on the spot.

The riper the fruit gets, the more fragile it is, leading to bruises and broken skin, but it is still very edible when it no longer looks beautiful.

Season
They start appearing in the markets in mid to late summer and continue through fall with their peak in September.

To soften
Leave the fruit out in your kitchen away from sunlight. It may take several weeks to soften so don't give up on it. The less ripening it has had on the tree, the more time it will take to soften and the earlier in the season it is, the longer it will take. They are ready when they yield to gentle pressure. Once ready to eat, you can store them in the refrigerator. If you feel the fruit needs washing, B.D. recommends that you wash and dry it while it is still hard since it becomes so fragile once it is ready to eat.

Flavor and texture
It is always difficult to describe the flavors of lesser known fruit. No one asks what an orange tastes like. What would you answer if someone who had never eaten any oranges asked you? "Well, hmm, it tastes like, umm, well, it's very juicy, it's somewhat acid and, well, let's see, it tastes like an orange."

What I would like to say is that a sapote tastes like a sapote. But that doesn't help you much, does it! It is a sweet fruit with perhaps a hint of banana flavor. It has a texture a bit like an avocado, quite custardy, actually. Its texture has led to names like "marmalade plum" and "custard apple". The cherimoya, as well, is commonly called the "custard apple" although the sapote actually resembles an apple in appearance whereas the cherimoya definitely does not.

Regarding the sweetness, B.D. says the fruit is so sweet that some people actually prefer the less yellow fruit which comes from the shadier side of the tree. You will need to try the variations for yourself to find what pleases your palate.

The skin is edible in all varieties. However, the greener varieties have a more sour skin which you may prefer not to eat.

The fruit have 1 to 3 seeds about the size of brazil nuts and may have some flat seeds as well. Discard these.

Using

This fruit is best eaten raw. Since it is custardy and fragile, it does not cook or freeze well. Try eating it fresh with a spoon or out of hand like an apple or pear. I like to mash the pulp and stir in a generous amount of lime juice. The flavors blend beautifully and the citrus prevents the sapote from turning brown.

RECIPE

Sapote Millet Pudding

    1 cup millet

    3 cups water

    3-4 ripe sapotes

    2 T maple syrup (optional)

Cook millet in water 1/2 hour or until done.
Remove seeds from sapote and mash.
Stir sapote and millet together and add maple syrup.

Serve warm or chilled.

B.D. Dautch

NOTES

STONE FRUITS

These fruits have a "stone" for a seed and include apricots, peaches, plums, nectarines and cherries.

Common traits

They are all summer fruit. The season is extended by way of the many different varieties and by the climate (cool or hot) where the fruit is grown.
They are all fragile with short shelf life.

Caution

I have noticed that many large growers of stone fruits tend to rush the season. I am sure they want to maximize the season, which is understandable. For the customer, however, this can mean great disappointment. I strongly recommend that at the start of the season you buy only one or two pieces of fruit initially to determine if the quality is satisfactory. You may need to wait as much as two to four weeks more before the fruit being brought to market is truly ready.

From the time an avocado reaches minimum maturity to the time it reaches maximum maturity is a span of many months. The fruit is satisfactory throughout this time, getting better and better with each passing week. In stone fruits, however, the time span from minimum to maximum maturity is extremely short. The grower needs to pick the fruit while it is still hard (for durability) but must be very careful to wait for the maximum amount of maturity possible before the fruit starts getting soft on the tree.

Picked too soon, the fruit will be nearly tasteless, is usually tart, and is likely to wrinkle rather than soften properly.

I visited Bill and Ruby Wilson at their farm in Pixley where they raise apricots, peaches, cherries, grapes, berries, melons and tomatoes. They both grew up on farms in Colorado. Bill has a degree in horticulture from Colorado A and M. He served in the Navy, farmed, taught agriculture to veterans, and spent one year working at a Colorado Fruit Research Station.

Then they moved to California where Bill had his own business selling seeds (alfalfa, barley) for many years before they "retired" to a ten acre property in Pixley. They planted the acreage with farmers' markets in mind, with diversified crops that they could sell directly to the consumer.

They also sell cover crops to grape growers in the Delano and Earlimart area.

Bill and Ruby work together in this farming venture and share the marketing workload. Saturday will often find one of their four married children and family helping with marketing activities. I enjoyed my visit to their farm immensely and they were a big help to me in the following information.

APRICOTS

Selecting

Looks can be deceiving. Do not judge by color. Varieties have been developed to achieve a beautiful ripe color more than a week before the fruit is ready.

Americans have developed the habit of judging produce quality strictly by its appearance, a habit encouraged by our food supply system where giant commercial producers ship giant quantities of product across many miles. It has to sit in field boxes, go through packing plants and loading docks, be shipped across country to supermarkets and survive this whole regimen looking edible to the consumer at the end of the line.

Royal Blenheim apricot

An apricot picked at its prime would never survive this grueling trip so hybrids are developed to look ripe before they actually are. How fortunate we are at our farmers' markets to be able to get our fruit at its prime right from the grower.

New England is very much in my being and I love every visit I make back there to see family, no matter what time of year. But I often think that the most difficult adjustment I would have to make if I were to move back there would not be to the humidity or bugs or long winter but rather to the lack of fine fresh produce all year long.

Back to apricot selection. Castlebright is an example of an apricot which will look ripe before it is. Bill and Ruby raise this variety and are careful to leave it on the tree until it actually **is** ripe, not just looking ripe.

Castlebright apricot

They also grow Royal Blenheims which Bill says are the ugliest apricots around but are the very best in flavor.

Look for

Aroma - As with muskmelon the fruit should have a scent that makes you want to eat it.

Softness - Apricots should have a softness to them. Avoid fruit that is still hard.

Sample - Buy a few pieces of fruit and taste test or ask the grower if you may have a sample.

134

Apricots picked at the proper degree of maturity can be eaten at the time you buy them. They can keep nicely for a number of days on your kitchen counter.

PEACHES and NECTARINES

O'Henry peach

Much the same holds true for peaches and nectarines as for apricots. Varieties have been developed to look ripe before they are so color is not a reliable test of ripeness.

Again, judge by aroma, especially in peaches, and softness. Peaches and nectarines can be much firmer than apricots when you purchase them but they do need to have achieved the proper degree of maturity. I would encourage the purchase of one or two pieces to taste test before buying in quantity. You may very well find that the ugliest fruit are the sweetest and most flavorful.

If you buy ripe fruit, it will be fragile, especially the peaches, and should be eaten very soon. If you buy the fruit still hard, let it soften to develop the best flavor.

PLUMS

Plums are very similar to the stone fruits we have already looked at but do have a few unique traits. They are quite sturdy compared to peaches and will store longer.

Again, color is only a partially reliable way to select this fruit because of hybrids developed to look ripe before they are mature. However, plums continue to darken in color as they soften so color can be a good indication of readiness to eat. The richest colored fruit in a container of any particular variety will be most ready to eat.

Flavor improves greatly with the softening process so be sure to have the patience to wait for them to get ripe.

CHERRIES

I am not aware of sour cherries being sold at our farmers' markets but we do have sweet cherries in abundance for a brief time of year. Cherry trees have high chilling requirements so they will not come from coastal or low desert areas.

A note for the future: horticulturists are always experimenting with the development of new varieties which are adapted to specific climates. Cherries are no exception and my husband and I have put in a Capulin cherry tree with low chill requirement. The fruit itself has large pits in proportion to the fruit and the flavor is

135

what I call "green". I like the fruit and it is very attractive so I am enjoying the experiment and expect to be trying it out at the market next year.

Season
Early Burlat will come into the market for about two weeks the first part of May.

Bing will appear the latter part of May and go into June.

Other varieties overlap these.

Selecting
In the case of cherries, color is a good indicator of quality and ripeness. Pick out the deepest colored fruit.

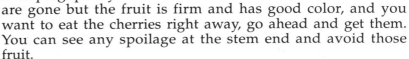

Bing cherry

Stems should be on for keeping quality. If the stems are gone but the fruit is firm and has good color, and you want to eat the cherries right away, go ahead and get them. You can see any spoilage at the stem end and avoid those fruit.

Lambert cherry

Rainier cherry

Some growers will have a lot of "twins" in their cherry boxes. Those grown in the hotter valley regions (Pixley, for instance, where Bill and Ruby Wilson raise their cherries) are affected by the heat during the previous summer when the fruit buds are differentiating in a way that produces double fruit. The flavor is not affected.

VEGETABLES

ARTICHOKES

When I started researching vegetables, I had the pleasure of visiting the Arroyo Grande farm of Lori and Kerry Nichols. Lori brewed coffee from freshly ground beans, and we sipped it while we sat at her kitchen table talking about all the crops they raise.

Lori and Kerry have been farming for about nine years. Their major crop is edible pod peas which they sell wholesale as well as at the farmers' market. But they also raise artichokes, beans, brussels sprouts, and berries. A new venture of theirs is blueberries, exciting for those of us in the southern portion of the state where we haven't had local blueberries before.

Although their farming operation is large, 200 acres, Lori and Kerry are still the ones behind their stand at the Santa Barbara Farmers' Market, and often you will get a glimpse of one of their three young sons.

I learned some interesting things from them about artichokes.

Varieties
Artichokes grown in the United States have all been the traditional globe varieties, some with thorns and some without. They are propagated with root cuttings and are perennial.

More recently, seedchokes have been introduced, very similar to the globe but they are raised from seed. They are thornless, more compact and more purple.

Season
Traditional globe artichokes are available for the most part two times a year, in spring as early as February and March and again in late summer/early fall. Growing practices can extend these two seasons. Seedchokes can be produced year round since they are grown from seed and plantings can be made year round.

Selecting
Whether the head is compact or open is of little consequence. These variations are caused by growing conditions. If they are widely open, they may be mature enough to be getting tough, but chances are that you won't run into this problem.

The quality of seedchokes is not as good as that of the traditional globe, one of those tradeoffs we make in order to have a fruit or vegetable year round.

Brown markings from frost on the tips and sides make artichokes look very sad but don't be deterred from buying them. Lori tells me that they have much better flavor as a result of the frost so you should select those if they are available.

Size is not a factor in selecting artichokes. All the small, medium, and large sizes have a fuzzy choke in the center, proportionate to the size of the artichoke, and preparation is the same regardless of size. The exception to this is newly-formed buds which should be only about an inch in diameter. At this point they have not yet developed the fuzzy choke in the center that the larger ones have and they are so young and soft that they can be eaten in their entirety after peeling off only the single outermost layer of leaves.

Flowers

Artichoke flowers are not edible but I mention them because you will often see the flowers at market after the edible artichoke season is past. Artichokes are actually flower buds and if allowed to grow, form quite magnificent blooms of purple which are lovely in fresh and dried arrangements.

ASPARAGUS

We had wild asparagus growing in the springlot on our farm and my mother used to watch for it to burst forth in the spring. It was slender and delicious and always available for only a short time.

Now field-grown asparagus is available for an extended period of time at some of our markets. Growers cut back or burn off the fern to encourage a second crop and they are learning how to time planting, harvesting, and pruning to yield nearly year round production.

Selecting
The cut end seals quickly after cutting but on fresh asparagus it will be white.

The stalks should be firm and crisp with no sign of the tip wilting when the bunch is held upright.

Diameter of the stalk is relatively unimportant. Some people believe there is no difference in tenderness or flavor between the different sizes. Others believe the larger stalks are more flavorful and one grower considers the very fat stalks gourmet quality. My own taste tests found no difference. Choose the size that suits your own preference and use.

Asparagus is sold with and without the "waste". If the waste of the lower end has been broken off, the asparagus is sold as "tips" and will be more expensive per pound since everything you are buying is edible. If the waste is still on, you will remove it at the time of preparation.

Color should be a healthy rich green. On tips this color should extend the whole length. On untrimmed stalks, the green will fade at the lower end to paler green and nearly white.

Preparation
For tips, simply wash and cook either whole or cut.

For stalks with the waste still on, there are more options. The stalk has a natural breaking point where the exterior becomes tough so simply snap it at this point. You now have tips to cook whole or cut and you have waste.

You can literally waste this portion, necessary if the stalks are very slender but not necessary if the stalks are fatter. Discard the lower portion of the stem where it is white. On the green portion which will be approximately 2" long, use your vegetable peeler to remove the tough outer skin. Cook the peeled center to eat as you do the tips, or cook and blend for asparagus soup.

C and G Produce in Lompoc recommends the following method of cooking whole tips. Stand bundle upright in kettle with lower ends standing in 1 to 2 inches of water. If your kettle is not deep enough, make a dome lid with aluminum foil. Steam 5-7 minutes.

Season
March through June typically. However, nearly year round at some markets.

CELERY

Celery is one of the more difficult vegetables to grow, requiring carefully controlled soil and temperature conditions for its first eight to nine weeks before the plants are large enough and sturdy enough to be transplanted into the field. Consequently, many vegetable growers rely on nurseries for celery seedlings rather than attempting to grow it from seed themselves.

Season all year

Selecting
Essentially, you want to get nice crisp stalks of medium size.

You will notice that some stalks are large and compact with the stems somewhat flattened and very snug to one another. Other times you will find stalks where the stems spread out and are quite rounded. The snug ones are usually lighter green and the more open ones dark green.

These traits are signs of different varieties and different seasons. They can also relate to the length of time the celery was allowed to grow.

The darker green stems are apt to be crisper but you won't notice any significant difference in flavor.

NOTES

CHAYOTE

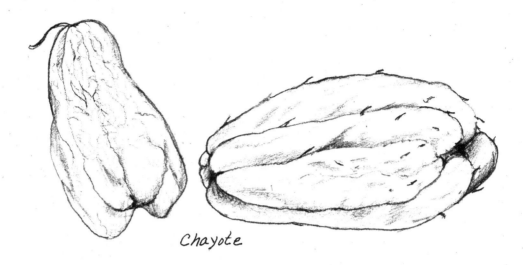

Chayote

Chayote (pronounced *chi* as in child, *yo* as in the toy Yo-Yo, *tay* to rhyme with ray) resembles summer squash in that it has a thin edible skin and a watery flesh. I use the word "watery" to distinguish these vegetables from the denser winter squash flesh. However, there is only one seed in chayote compared to the numerous seeds of summer squash.

Chayote has its own unique shape, broader at the bottom and narrower at the stem end, a bit like a huge pear that has been flattened side to side a little. The surface has deep lengthwise rumples. The color of chayote ranges from dark to light green. The younger it is, the darker the green, the more mature it is, the lighter the green.

The surface can be very smooth or it can be covered with numerous spines.

Season
Generally, chayote is available during summer and fall when squash is available. However, in warmer areas, it can be found for a more extended time.

Selecting
Size is not a factor. Color is not especially important either. Do look at the blossom (bottom) end for signs of the seed protruding. If the seed does not show, the skin is tender and very edible. If the seed shows, the chayote is very mature with a tougher skin and will need to be peeled before cooking. Avoid a chayote if the seed is not only protruding but sending out little roots as well. These roots derive their nourishment from the chayote flesh, thus reducing the quality of the flesh.

Using

Chayote is always cooked. If the seed does not show, cut into quarters, slice, or dice and cook the entire vegetable. If the seed shows, peel before or after cooking. Chayote holds it shape nicely after cooking which makes it a more versatile vegetable than summer squash.

It can be steamed or simmered, fried, or baked. Cooked diced chayote can be added to tossed salads.

Storage

Chayote can be stored for quite some time in a cool place.

CORN

There are numerous varieties of corn which can be divided by size into standard and bantam and by color into yellow, white and bi-color, also called calico.

Selecting

Whether you choose yellow, white, or bi-color is a purely personal preference. White corn is sweeter and more tender than yellow corn but some people find yellow corn heartier and richer in flavor. The older ones among us may have childhood memories that make yellow corn the only corn!

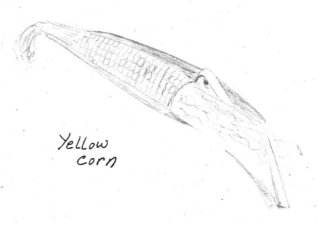

Yellow
Corn

Myth: all the kernels must line up in absolutely even rows. Reality: Crooked kernels are just as good as straight ones.

There are several ways to judge corn *without* opening it. (See growers' pet peeves later in this chapter.)

1. The cob should feel firm and full in your hand.

2. Rub your thumb from a couple inches below the tip to the tip. This lets you know whether or not the ear is full its entire length. If you find a ridge and the tip is flexible, the kernels at the end are not developed but you can get a very accurate feel of the maturity of the rest of the kernels by the contrast.

3. The tassel or corn silk should be brown. Green or tan indicates an immature ear which will be lacking in substance and flavor. Very dark brown, verging on black, indicates a very mature ear which some people find to be too tough. However, other people consider this the very best.

4. The color of the husk should be a healthy green.

5. Judge the overall quality of produce and reliability of the grower. His reputation may be the best guide to the quality of his corn. A grower who values high quality is careful to pick only ripe corn to bring to his customers.

Worms

Worms (we commonly call them worms, but they are actually caterpillars) and corn go together. There is no way around it and you simply expect some loss.

Conventionally-grown corn treated to control worms will be mostly worm-free but there will be an occasional ear inhabited by one of those wriggly creatures.

If you buy organic corn, most ears will host a worm. As soon as you get home, open each ear enough to remove the worm. The longer they are inside those ears, the more of your dinner they will devour before you get to it!

Note: There are some ears in any large batch of organic corn which will be free of worms. However, if you get all or mostly worm-free corn from a grower who claims to be organic, you should be skeptical and ask how he controls worms.

There are organic means of controlling worms but they are very labor intensive. Oil must be put in the corn silk of each ear to smother the eggs.

Lori and Kerry Nichols find that worms prefer yellow corn to white corn, so you may find that you have less loss if you opt for white.

Using
The most important thing to know about corn is that the sugar starts turning to starch as soon as the corn is picked. Therefore, it should be eaten as soon as possible after picking as it loses flavor and sweetness with each passing hour and day.

There are a few varieties which hold sugar content and flavor a little better than others but a good rule of thumb is to eat any corn as soon as possible. If you want to hold the corn a day or two, husk and place it in the refrigerator. The husking and the chill both slow the change of sugar to starch.

RECIPES

Laure Kendrick was the first manager of the Carpinteria Farmers' Market which was opened with great success in 1989. Her husband, Craig, raises corn to sell there and at the Santa Barbara market, and she strongly recommends that corn be cooked only one minute rather than the usual three to five.

Bring the water to a boil, put corn in all at once, cover and cook one minute.

Alice Pearce says microwaving is also an excellent method of cooking fresh corn. Simply place the ears with husk on a paper towel in the microwave. Cook on high four minutes, slightly longer for each additional ear.

For ease in removing the husk from hot cooked corn, cut off the stem end and the silk end at the first row of kernels before cooking. Serve the corn in the husk, and it will stay hot until eaten.

Growers' pet peeves in the corn department
The Ripper. This is the person (most of us?) who open twenty ears of corn to find the perfect half dozen. The corn starts to dry out as soon as it is open and other customers don't want to buy it, which creates a substantial loss to the grower.

The Puncturer. This is the person who punctures the kernels to see if milky fluid bursts forth. Please don't puncture kernels with your fingernail and then put the ear down. Again, this leads to loss for the grower who cannot sell damaged goods.

Depending on the individual grower and the health department in the county where the market is being held, you may be able to have a sample piece of the corn to verify freshness.

Miniature corn

This is a relatively new idea, tiny ears which you eat raw, cob as well as kernels. You can purchase baby ears which are immature regular corn and you can purchase specialty varieties which have been developed to be small. This corn is more durable than regular corn and will keep quite nicely in the husk in the refrigerator for several days.

Miniature corn

Serving Ideas

Hors D'Oeuvre: The very tiny cobs can be used with a yogurt, sour cream or cheese dip.

Lori Nichols

Salads: Add the very tiny version to salads whole. Slice the larger varieties crosswise and toss into salad.

Lori Nichols

NOTES

CRUCIFEROUS VEGETABLES

These are all members of the mustard family which provides us with a fair number of our year round vegetables. It is interesting that most of the vegetables which can be grown year round are botanically vegetables, that is, we are eating parts of the plant other than the fruit. Fruiting is a summer and fall activity of plants so vegetables which are botanically fruits are generally not available in the winter. Winter squash and edible pod peas are notable exceptions.

Ron Labastida and his brothers of Labastida Brothers Farms in Santa Maria grow many varieties of our cruciferous vegetables. Ron has been a great help to me on this chapter, and I am lucky to have his stand right across from mine at the Santa Barbara market. The result is that I have been able to cook with the more unusual crucifers as well as the common ones.

Ron's father was a young village fisherman in the Philippine Islands when a typhoon tossed his boat at sea for several days, finally leaving him on an island. After that experience, his family urged him to find a different life. In 1928, at the age of eighteen, he came to the United States and found his way to Santa Maria.

While Ron was growing up, his father farmed 20-30 acres, selling produce from farm stands and directly to grocery stores. In the meantime Ron and his brothers grew up and pursued other interests, but when their father retired in 1975, they returned to Santa Maria to take over the farming operation. However, since there were now four families to support, they expanded.

Today, three brothers farm approximately 425 acres. With this larger operation, they broker much of their product but still continue the family tradition of selling directly to stores and directly to the consumer by way of our farmers' markets. They have sold at as many as nine market sites in a season.

Most of their farming uses conventional methods but 25 acres are certified organic and Ron is president of his local chapter of the CCOF. They are very honest at their stands about which product is organic and which is not, a trait I value highly since it allows me to make educated decisions.

CABBAGE

There are three basic types of cabbage, each with many varieties. **Solid round heads** come in light green and red. They are usually quite heavy and compact with the leaves tightly layered.

Savoy is also a round head green cabbage but the leaves are crinkly and the outer leaves curl a bit.

Chinese or *Napa* cabbage is always barrel shaped or cylindrical rather than round. Often the leaves are crinkly and they can be rather loose or tightly layered. Some varieties are fatter and heavier, and others longer and more slender. They come in various shades of green and the leaves become lighter in color toward the center of the head. They are somewhat lighter in flavor than round heads.

Season all year.

Selecting
Look for heads which are fresh looking and free of blemishes. Heavier heads are more dense so there is a great deal more cabbage in one of those than there is in a loose head of the same size. The loose head can have just as fine a flavor but keep in mind that it won't have the same number of servings.

Using
Cabbages are versatile and can be used raw and cooked.

KALE

Kale comes to market as individual stems tied into bunches rather than a head like the other crucifers. The leaves are very curly, gray-green in color and very sturdy. They have a distinct cruciferous look to them. There is a very pretty variety called Red Russian with red-edged leaves which are flatter and less curly than the traditional varieties. The whole plant is pulled like spinach so there will be a number of small plants in each bundle.

Season all year but most plentiful during the cooler months.

Selecting
Kale is hardy so you should not have any trouble getting fresh, perky, unblemished bunches.

Using
They are best cooked and because of their sturdy quality, they hold their shape nicely rather than wilting like most cooked greens.

RECIPE
Kale Soup

1 small bunch fresh kale

1 large or 2 medium onions

4 c water or chicken stock

salt and pepper to season

Wash and cut kale leaves into bite size pieces, discarding lower stem. Dice onion. Add both vegetables to water or chicken stock and simmer until tender, about 8 minutes. Season to suit your own taste. Serve piping hot.

ORNAMENTAL CABBAGES AND KALES
(Flowering Kale)

These crucifers are loose open heads which look like beautiful large flowers. The leaves are curly and very decorative. They come in many different varieties with numerous colors and shadings. The colors become more brilliant in the cool winter months. They can be used as flowers if you like but they are also edible.

Season all year

Selecting
They should be fresh-looking and free of blemishes.

Using
They are usually used raw since other crucifers have better flavor cooked than these do. The small leaves can be added to salads whole, the larger ones cut. If you like, you can blanch them first to make them a little more tender.

The different colored leaves make lovely garnishes and can turn your ordinary dish into a showpiece.

BRUSSELS SPROUTS

Brussels sprouts

Lori and Kerry Nichols sell a great many brussels sprouts at the farmers' market. Of all the vegetables they raise, brussels sprouts bring the most questions. What are they? What do you do with them? How do they grow?

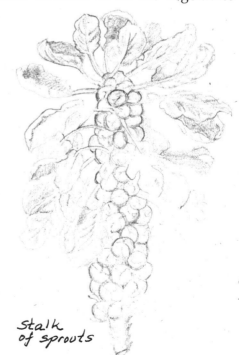

stalk of sprouts

They are a tiny vegetable resembling a cabbage and are, of course, in the same family. However, they need to be cooked and they have their own distinct flavor.

Some people envision a tidy row of miniature cabbages growing in the garden but in reality these little vegetables grow on large stalks with many sprouts on each one. The sprouts on each stalk graduate in size from largest at the bottom to smallest at the top.

Season November through February

Selecting
Lori suggests that the smaller ones may be a bit more tender than the large ones but the flavor is equally good no matter what the size. Avoid any so large that they are starting to split.

I asked about the bitterness that always seems to be present in the ones I have had from the supermarket. She believes cold storage and the resultant aging is the cause. I haven't done a scientific experiment to find out for sure, but I do know that the freshly picked sprouts that the Nichols bring to the market are never bitter.

Most often sprouts have been removed from the stalk and are sold loose. You might want to select sprouts uniform in size so they cook evenly.

Whole stalks
Lori and Kerry sell whole stalks as well. These are not only intriguing but they are practical. Hung upside down in a dry place they can store for up to 3 months. The sprouts get the nourishment and moisture they need from the stalk so they do not need to be frozen or put in cold storage in your refrigerator.

Use the largest sprouts first and work your way along the stem to the smallest.

If you don't plan to store the stalk, you can even eat the leaves at the top which resemble a loose head of cabbage. Discard the outer leaves and use the heart. They can be used raw or cooked.

New variety
Brussels sprouts have always been green. Now there is a new variety which is red. They are exactly like green ones in all respects except color.

Cooking
They can either be steamed or dropped into boiling water for about 10 minutes depending upon the size of the individual sprouts.

Decorating idea
Use a stalk as a centerpiece for your dining table, filling the spaces between the sprouts with baby's breath and dried flowers. One of Lori's customers did this and I am sorry I don't have his name to give him credit for such a good idea.

You might want to buy a stalk of the new red variety, tie on a bold red bow and hang it on your front door at Christmas.

BOK CHOY
(Pak choi)

Another name for this vegetable is Chinese chard cabbage which helps describe its appearance. It is a loose cluster of beautiful green leaves atop fresh white or light green bold stalks. It is usually broad at the base where the stalks overlap, and then tapers into its narrowest point just before the leaves burst forth.

There are many varieties of bok choy but the most common ones at our markets have broad thick white stalks topped with dark green leaves. They vary in size from very small, about 6", to standard large sizes, more than a foot in length.

Season all year.

Selecting
Look for perky leaves, a very fresh look and no blemishes on stalks or leaves.

Using
The entire bok choy is edible, the only waste being a thin slice off the bottom end at time of preparation. It can be eaten raw or cooked. The stalks are crisp and very mild in flavor. The leaves give a hint of their relative, the mustard.

If you purchase the very small ones, they can be steamed whole. You might want to try standing them upright with stalks in water and leaves in steam.

Larger varieties should be broken apart. The stalks take longer to cook so start them first, boiling or steaming for 2 to 3 minutes. Then add leaves and continue cooking for another 2 to 3 minutes.

Besides eating plain, they can be added to soups, stir-fried, or used in any way your imagination takes you.

KOHLRABI

Here is an interesting crucifer with a shape quite different from all the others. The large bulb is actually the stem of the plant and the leaves come out all around it on the upper half.

Season winter/spring

Selecting
Generally, smaller, younger kohlrabi will be the most tender. Since growers are always experimenting with new varieties and since there is a giant kohlrabi, it is possible that some markets might have this variety. It can be 10" in diameter and is supposed to be superior in quality.

The vegetable should be firm and the leaves be perky and green. Yellowing leaves indicate that it was picked some time ago and is no longer fresh.

Using
The kohlrabi bulb can be eaten raw in salads or with dips. It can be cooked in stews, soups, and used in stir-frying. It should be peeled, which can be done before or after cooking. Use the leaves in soups.

BROCCOLI

With all the crucifers we've looked at so far, it is the leaves and stems that we eat. Broccoli, however, is a dense head of flower buds on a sturdy thick stalk.

Season all year

Selecting
The buds should be tightly closed and a rich green in color. The stems should be crisp.

If the buds are starting to look pale and/or the stems are feeling rubbery, it means that the head was picked some time ago and is getting old. Avoid these.

If the buds are beginning to open, it means that the head was picked later in its development. You are not likely to find heads like this at our farmers' markets. It is the home gardener who finds himself with too many heads ready to harvest at one time who has to let some grow a bit longer.

Using
Besides all the usual ways of using this vegetable, try peeling the lower stem and using the center in cole slaw or diced into a tossed salad.

When using broccoli for an hors d'oeuvre, with dips, or in salads, blanch it first. Blanching gives it a magnificent green color and makes it easier to eat while still keeping it essentially raw.

CAULIFLOWER

Cauliflower is a creamy white head of tightly closed buds known as a "curd".

Season all year

Selecting
It is easy to select the highest quality of this vegetable. The curd should be completely fresh and white. As it ages, it develops dark spots.

BROCCOFLOWER
(Cauli-broc, Brocauli, Green cauliflower)

This crucifer is a cross between broccoli and cauliflower and the name "Broccoflower" is actually a trademark name of Tanimura and Antle, a large grower-shipper based in Salinas. It is used in the same way we use the name "Kleenex" to mean any tissue or "Xerox" to mean any photocopy.

Both the appearance and flavor are a true blend of the two. The color is pale purple-green. The flavor is heartier than cauliflower and milder than broccoli. Be sure to try this delicious new hybrid.

In talking to Ron, I learned that growing this hybrid is a challenge at any time of the year. Quality is superior in winter, less good in warmer weather.

Season all year

Selection and Use
Same as for broccoli and cauliflower.

BROCCOLI RAAB
(Rapini)

This crucifer is one of the newer varieties at our markets. It looks a bit like long-stemmed miniature broccoli heads and comes to market tied in bunches.

Season all year

Selection and Use
From Ron, I learned that this vegetable is labor-intensive to grow. It must be picked after the buds form but before they start to open and that time span is very short, especially in summer. When selecting, be sure to look for the same tight bud system that you look for in broccoli. Use the same way as broccoli or broccoflower.

NOTES

CUCUMBERS

Cucumbers are divided into two basic groups, salad or slicing and pickling.

Salad varieties
There are three distinct types of salad cucumbers. The most common are quite smooth-skinned, straight, and average 6 to 9 inches in length. The size and number of seeds varies according to variety. They are normally sold green.

Another type of salad cucumber is the very long slender Armenian or Japanese variety, also sold green.

The third type is known as lemon cucumber which gets its name from its shape and color, not its flavor. These cucumbers are quite round and are either pale yellow-green or yellow. Because of their shape and size, and very crisp texture, they make a delightful snack eaten out of hand.

Pickling varieties
These cucumbers are smaller than the typical salad varieties, always with small seeds and very crisp texture. They tend to curve and taper in strange ways and to have little bumps and burrs. They are generally light green, often a blend of green and cream.

Selecting
All varieties should be crisp.

Color is important as it relates to maturity. All cucumbers are actually yellow when they are mature, but, with the exception of lemon cucumbers, they are sold in an immature green state. When green, the skin and seeds are edible. If the cucumber is showing signs of yellow, it is still very edible but plan on peeling it and removing the seeds.

Lemon cucumbers are sold at the young pale yellow-green stage and in their mature yellow stage as well. Either way is fine. The more mature darker ones have thicker, and therefore tougher, skins which can be eaten or removed according to individual preference. The seeds do not need to be removed in either case.

Size is not a factor in choosing cucumbers.

Using
Cucumbers are usually eaten raw or pickled. They can be peeled or not according to taste. They can also be made into delicious soups, usually served chilled.

If you should come across ripe cucumbers, large yellow ones, you can peel, remove the seeds and dice into salads or eat plain. If you like pickles, you might want to try the ripe cucumber pickle recipe that follows.

RECIPES

I have fond memories of helping my mother make pickles from our own homegrown cucumbers when I was very young. We stored quarts and quarts of them in the cellar. Sour pickles were the favorite of one brother and saccharine pickles (war time sugar rationing) were my favorite. We used to pack jars with fresh slices for dill pickles, and soaked crisp slices in a kitchen sink full of salt water overnight in preparation for bread and butter pickles.

Following are two of my mother's recipes.

Ripe Cucumber Pickles

7 pounds cubed ripe cucumber (peel and seeds removed)

Boil until tender. Drain.

Bring to a boil:

> 1 pt white vinegar
>
> 3 1/2 pounds sugar
>
> 1/2 t oil of cloves
>
> 1/2 t oil of cinnamon

Pour over cucumbers and let stand overnight.

In AM pour off juice, bring to boil, and pour over cukes again.

Next AM, bring cucumbers *and* juice just to boil and put into hot sterilized jars.

Gladness Luce

Dill Pickles

This recipe for dill pickles is my mother's favorite and she used it for many years.

Wash and dry cucumbers and put into jars. Cover with 2 grape leaves and a sprig of dill. Fill jars with brine and seal.

Brine: (enough for 4 to 5 qts)

> 2 qts water boiled and cooled
>
> 1 pt cider vinegar
>
> 1/2 c salt
>
> 1/4 t cream of tartar

Let stand at least six weeks before using.

Gladness Luce

EDIBLE GOURDS

Most gourds are decorative and inedible but there are several varieties which are outstanding vegetables. They are used primarily in Asian cooking but with the help of our farmers' markets, they are becoming more widely used. They have been one of my delicious discoveries in the making of this book.

BITTER MELON
(Chinese Bitter Melon, Foo Gwa)

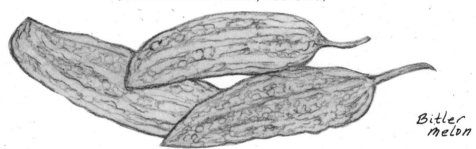

Bitter
melon

This vegetable gourd is an important part of Chinese cooking but not well-known to the rest of us. Because of its name, I had been reluctant to try it, but it was a delightful surprise!

Bitter melon is a light green vegetable, waxy in appearance with a deeply rumpled surface. It resembles a regular cucumber in shape and size.

Season Summer and fall

Selecting
Bitter melon is straightforward. It must be green without any signs of the orange color which it develops as it matures. It should be firm and free of blemishes. Select the size that best meets your purpose.

Storing
Treat like summer squash. Eat as soon as possible but storage in the refrigerator for several days will not impair the quality.

Using
Remove a bit from each end, cut in half lengthwise and scoop out the seeds and pith. The peel is left on. It can be eaten raw but is usually cooked. They can be stuffed, stir fried, steamed, and used in chutney.

Add raw to tossed salad in small quantities to give an unusual and very nice flavor accent.

I had heard varying opinions about the bitterness in relation to cooking time so I diced a whole melon into my fry pan with a bit of oil. After sauteing just long enough to heat the melon through, I removed a portion and found that it tasted very much like raw green beans but with a touch of bitterness, not unpleasant.

I continued to saute the rest of the melon until it was soft, removed some and found it no more or less bitter. I sauteed the remainder of the melon until it was nicely browned. Again, the bitterness didn't change, but the flavor resulting from this cooking period was my favorite. It was remarkably like that of fried green tomatoes.

I put some in a homemade chicken soup and found it a delightful flavor addition. The recipe follows.

RECIPE
Chicken Soup

1 small fryer chicken, cut up

2 medium size yellow onions, cut in quarters

1 stalk celery, sliced

salt & pepper to taste

1 c corn

1/4 - 1/2 c bitter melon sauteed until brown

Place fryer in 4 qt. pot. Add onions, celery, seasoning and water to cover. Simmer until chicken is done. Remove chicken from broth and allow to cool enough to handle. Save the breast and thighs for main dishes. Remove meat from other pieces and put back in broth. Cut onion into bite sized pieces. If corn is fresh or frozen, add and cook. Then add sauteed bitter melon. If corn is canned, add at same time as bitter melon. Bring to simmering point and serve.

LUFFA
(Loofah, Cee gwa, Petola, Chinese okra)

Luffa has many names depending upon one's ethnic background and can be found at our markets under all the names I have listed above.

This gourd comes in two varieties. *Angled luffa* is darker green and elongated, slightly larger at the bottom and tapering into a graceful curving neck. It is covered by vertical ribs which give rise to the name "Chinese okra".

The other variety is lighter green, *smooth luffa* (lacking the ribs) but showing darker green markings where the ribs might be. It has a larger diameter than the ribbed luffa and tapers gently toward the stem end, staying quite straight.

If left on the vine to mature, this smooth variety of luffa can be washed and dried to become the luffa bath sponge.

162

Angled luffa

Luffa is a recent discovery on my part and a delightful one. Slices look much like slices of cucumber, moist and crisp with small seeds. There is a resemblance to summer squash as well but the flavor is much sweeter than squash or cucumber which makes it a more versatile vegetable.

Season Summer and fall

Selecting
It is vital that this vegetable be purchased in an immature state but it is easy to select high quality luffa. Go by feel. The vegetable should be very firm. If it feels at all spongy, it will be spongy on the inside too.

Storing
Treat like summer squash.

Using
Using a knife, scrape down each rib to remove the tough edge on the angled luffa. There is no need to remove the entire depth of the ribs and no need to peel either variety. It is now ready for eating raw in salads, with dips or simply plain.

It can also be cooked, steamed like summer squash or added to any number of dishes.

I like the challenge of creating recipes for fruits or vegetables that are new to me and I offer two recipes for this delightful vegetable.

RECIPES

Chicken Vegetable Soup

4 c chicken stock

1 c leftover chicken

1 large onion

1 or 2 carrots

1 luffa

pepper and salt as desired

Cut onion into bite size pieces, slice carrots and luffa. Add vegetables to chicken stock and simmer until just barely tender. Add cut up chicken and seasoning. Heat just to simmering point and serve.

Chocolate Luffa Cake

1/2 c margarine	2 1/2 c unsifted flour
1/2 c oil	5 T cocoa
1 1/4 c sugar	1 t baking powder
2 eggs	1 t soda
1 t vanilla	1/2 t cinnamon
1/2 c sour milk	1/2 t cloves
2 c finely chopped luffa	

Cream margarine, oil, and sugar together. Add eggs, vanilla, and milk. Beat thoroughly. Mix dry ingredients together, add to moist ingredients. Mix well but do not beat. Last, add luffa. Bake in greased 10 x 13 cake pan at 325° for 35 - 40 min.

I purchased a spongy luffa to compare its quality to that of a young firm luffa. The interior was getting dry and the skin was tougher. After scraping the ribs off, I chopped it fine and made this cake with it. I gave samples to friends to get their evaluation. The tough skin became chewy bits throughout the cake and everyone seemed to enjoy it.

Ideally, the cake should be made with a firm luffa, but, if you find yourself with a spongy one that won't be good for such things as salad or soup, don't waste it. It still makes an excellent cake.

HAIRY MELON

Hairy melons are actually immature winter melons and can be round, cylindrical or in the case of the *jointed melon*, cylindrical with a narrowing mid-way along the length. They are covered with fine hairs and are usually light green.

Season Summer and fall

Selecting
Since these melons lose their hairy covering as they mature, you will want to choose melons with a good covering of fine hairs. Size will be up to 8″. They should be firm and free of blemishes.

Storing
Treat like summer squash.

Using
You can peel the melons but that really isn't necessary since you can simply rub the hairs off. They can be diced or sliced and cooked in a number of different ways, much like summer squash. They can be steamed, stir-fried, and even stuffed if you hollow them out.

WINTER MELON
(Winter Gourd, Doan Gwa, Wax Gourd)

There are different varieties of winter melons, varying in shape from very round to cylindrical with blunt ends. They vary widely in size as well, from very small immature fruit of just a few inches to giant melons as much as two to four feet in length and 100 pounds or more in weight.

Some of the smaller varieties which have furry skin when immature are sold at the market as hairy melon.

Other varieties are sold at maturity when they are very large and have a waxy coating on the skin and are sold as winter melons.

Season Summer through winter

Selecting
This melon will be green with a whitish waxy coating. Select the size that suits your purpose.

Storing
The waxy coating provides excellent keeping quality. Store in a cool place, each gourd separate from one another for up to half a year.

Using
The mature winter melon has a milder flavor than the immature hairy melon. Cut into manageable pieces for peeling, remove peel and seeds, then slice or cube for use in soups, stews, and stir-frying. Winter melon can also be pickled.

Firm-fleshed varieties are used for Chinese winter melon soup, an impressive dish in which the soup ingredients are placed in the melon and the whole is steamed until done. When the soup is served, pieces of melon are scooped out and added to each serving.

NOTES

EGGPLANT

There are a number of varieties available at our California markets. The large dark purple variety grown commercially is common. But as our markets have proliferated and expanded, so have the varieties of eggplant. The slender dark purple Japanese eggplant has become very common. Light purple, white round and elongated varieties and round creamy white with green stripes are easy to find. They are all mild in flavor and used the same way.

Season summer into fall. It needs heat to grow well.

Selecting
Choose smooth, shiny-skinned eggplants with a fresh perky calyx (the leaf-like area around the stem). Heavy weight for the size is a good indicator of high quality but size itself is not important as long as the eggplant is mature. Judge maturity by rich color.

An immature eggplant will be green under the skin. Although you can't see this until you start using it, you can become aware of the exterior appearance on such immature fruit to help you in judging in the future. If you feel unsure about making a selection, ask the grower to help you.

I have tried eggplant of the Japanese variety that look magnificent, shiny, smooth, firm and without scars. I have tried others of the same variety that look quite the worse for wear and have sat around awhile. My husband helped me with taste testing and the bottom line was that there really wasn't any difference!

Get the freshest, best-looking eggplant you can find, but if you arrive at the end of the market with your heart set on eggplant and the only ones left are sad-looking, go ahead and give them a try.

Using
There is not a great deal of difference among the varieties in terms of flavor. The white varieties are a bit firmer and have a slightly tougher skin. This means they hold their shape better when cooked.

You can use all the varieties interchangeably.

RECIPE

Fried Eggplant

Here is a serving suggestion from David Avila who raises both eggplant and pecans. Instead of coating slices with flour prior to frying, coat them with pecan meal.

NOTES

FENNEL
(Anise)

The fennel sold at our markets is a different variety than that which grows wild throughout California. The wild variety has slender stems so it is the leaves that are used as an herb and the seeds for seasoning.

In our market variety, the stems are greatly enlarged at the base and overlap to form a "bulb". In both varieties the leaves are feathery and resemble dill in appearance. There is a distinct scent to this vegetable which reminds people of licorice or anise.

Season
Fennel is a cool weather vegetable and will start appearing in the markets about November and December. It is in great abundance in January and will continue to be available into late spring.

Selecting
The feathery leaves should be very green and fresh. The bulb should be white, crisp, and unblemished. If the outer layers of the bulb are starting to dry or are damaged, you will need to discard them or at least the defective parts of them. Since the outermost layers are the thickest, such damage means you can have a fair amount of waste.

Storing
Remove stems just above the bulb, place in a plastic bag and store in the vegetable drawer of the refrigerator for up to a week.

Using
This is an absolutely delicious and versatile vegetable. Don't let the anise scent discourage you from trying it. The flavor is quite mild.

Cut the stems off just above the bulb and wash thoroughly. The leaves are used as an herb seasoning and as a garnish. The bulb is used in many ways and can be eaten raw or cooked. The bulb can be cut in any direction you wish, depending upon your use. There is a little heart in the center bottom which holds the layers together if you cut them lengthwise into wedges.

I include several recipes to show how versatile fennel is and I hope they will inspire you to venture out on your own.

RECIPES

Open-Face Fennel Sandwich

Whole grain bread

Fennel

Red bell pepper

Sharp cheddar cheese

Toast slice of bread. Cut fennel crosswise in 1/4 inch slices and place one large or two small slices on toast to cover surface. Cover fennel with thin slices of ripe red bell pepper. Grate or thinly slice cheese to cover entire top of sandwich. Place in microwave on medium heat for 1 minute or just until cheese melts. (Do not let cheese bubble.) Eat!

Fennel Potato Bake

4 medium potatoes

2 fennel bulbs

olive or canola oil

pepper if desired

Lightly oil bottom of large shallow casserole. Wash potatoes and fennel. Slice potatoes into 1/4 inch slices. Slice fennel crosswise into 1/4 inch slices. Layer the two vegetables in the casserole. Brush lightly with oil. Pepper to suit. Bake uncovered 30 minutes at 425°. Top should be crisp.

Meatball Fennel Stew

1 pound lean ground beef	3 medium potatoes
1 slice whole grain bread	2 onions
1 egg	28 oz. can stewed tomatoes
1 medium fennel bulb	

Wet slice of bread and squeeze out excess water. Mix ground beef, bread, and egg together. Form into 1" meatballs. Fry. In the meantime prepare fennel, potatoes and onions by cutting into chunks. Simmer until tender in small amount of water. Add tomatoes and heat. Add meatballs and allow the whole to simmer briefly before serving.

GREENS

When I was a girl living on our farm in Vermont, we had a huge garden every summer. We had the usual greens like lettuce, chard and beet greens. But my mother also liked to try new things which she heard about by way of the neighbors. It is important to know that in those days and in my family, one had to eat a little of everything that was served, and one had to clean up everything on one's plate.

We sat down one sunny summer's evening to a dinner that included wild milkweed greens. I took my first bite. A fuzzy furry mass lodged in my mouth. Shudders went through my slender body and I sat there frozen. My siblings were made of stronger stuff than I because one by one they cleaned their plates and were excused. I, however, sat there and sat there and sat there still longer. I couldn't eat the greens and they wouldn't vanish!

The problem lay in the fact that my mother had picked the first leaves of the second crop instead of the first leaves of the first crop. I've never heard of milkweed in California so you probably won't have to worry about getting these furry greens but there are many, many wonderful other greens.

Storage of most greens is the same so I explain it here at the start. Wash leaves thoroughly to remove all dirt and sand. Shake excess water off. Wrap in paper or cloth towel and place inside plastic bag. Store in refrigerator.

The plastic bag, which doesn't breathe, holds moisture in the package and prevents wilting and drying out. But the very fact that it doesn't breathe means that damp leaves directly in contact with it will rot much faster. Thus, we use the towel which breathes and serves to control the moisture next to the greens.

LETTUCE

There are numerous kinds of lettuce. There is, of course, the familiar iceberg head lettuce so common in the supermarket. This is available at farmers' markets but the vast majority of lettuce varieties will be of the leafy kind.

I have thought of listing the various kinds but there are so many varieties with new ones being introduced every year that the information could form a little book all on its own. Instead, we will talk in generalities.

Season all year

Selecting

Generally speaking, the thicker the lettuce leaf, the more durable it is. The thinner and more delicate the leaf, the less durable it is. Romaine lettuce is the most hardy. Oak leaf lettuce is one of the most fragile.

Keeping this in mind, you might want to purchase several kinds, using the more delicate early in your week and saving the hardier for later in the week. Try different kinds to find your favorites and try mixing bronze and green colors in the same salad.

The leaves should be very fresh and perky. A small grower will have picked his lettuce the day of the market or the day before for a morning market but no earlier. It will not be iced although it will have been chilled overnight if picked the day before.

Large growers will pick their lettuce further ahead of the market and will bring it to the market in cartons containing ice to keep the lettuce in top quality.

One way to determine how long ago the lettuce was picked is to look at the bottom of the stem end. If it is moist and greenish white, it was just picked. The longer it has been picked, the dryer and darker the end will become until it eventually turns brown.

Using

Wash thoroughly to remove all dirt and sand.

Little creatures sometimes lurk in the lettuce if no pesticides have been used.

> Slugs: These are like snails without shells and they bury in between the snug folds of the leaves. If left in the head they will continue to eat and leave their droppings. Simply remove them and wash the leaves well.

> Aphids: These are minute insects which can be found over the surface of the leaves where they blend in so well with the leaf color that you may not notice them. A good washing is the way to remove them.

ENDIVE

Endive is another salad green, one from the chicory family. It grows like leaf lettuce and is usually picked as a whole head like the lettuces. It has beautiful curly leaves, darker green outside and lighter green as you go to the center of the head. It is usually somewhat bitter but variety and growing conditions affect this trait and I have found endive at the market which is scarcely bitter at all.

Season all year

Using
Wash thoroughly to remove all sand and dirt and break a generous amount into tossed salad for a flavor accent.

RECIPE

Endive Salad

1 medium head endive, cut into bite size pieces

1/4 pound bacon

1/3 c vinegar

1/3 c sugar

Cook bacon. Drain and save grease. Crumble bacon and mix with grease, vinegar and sugar. Shake well and mix into endive.

If you prefer not to eat the bacon grease, substitute vegetable oil. You can also try fake bacon bits and oil in place of the bacon and grease.

RADICCHIO

Like endive, this salad green is also a member of the chicory family and therefore has the slightly bitter taste we associate with the chicories. Most varieties form loose heads with leaves of red and cream.

Season all year

Selecting
As with all greens, look for fresh crisp heads free of blemishes.

Using
Wash thoroughly and break leaves up into salad for flavor accent. The beautiful color adds great appeal to a green salad. The leaves also make a lovely garnish.

ARUGULA

This leafy green is sometimes known as *rocket* and is related to mustard. It has a spicy, nutty flavor and is added to salad in a lesser quantity than lettuce but in greater quantity than an herb. The winter leaves are slightly milder than the summer leaves, less mature leaves are milder than mature leaves.

Season
It is available year round. In spring and summer it is susceptible to flea beetles which make tiny holes in the leaves. These holes detract from the appearance but do not affect the use of the green. The beetles can be controlled by a cloth covering the

crop, physically preventing the insects from getting to the plants. They can also be controlled with sprays which meet organic standards as well as conventional regulations.

Storing

Store arugula just as you store herbs. Be sure it is quite dry, close in a plastic bag, and place in the refrigerator.

MACHES
(Corn Salad, Lambs Lettuce)

Maches is a small leafy green, the largest leaves being about the size of a tablespoon. The plant is a cluster of 10-15 leaves which grow close to the ground in a rather horizontal fashion, making harvesting more tedious than it is for most of the other greens. It has a mild, nutlike, very delicious flavor.

Season cool weather

Selecting

The leaves come to market in packets of individual leaves or loose in tubs. Look for fresh perky leaves.

Using

Add a generous amount to your tossed salad. If you are feeling extravagant, make your whole salad of just this one green.

SPINACH

Spinach is a delicious green, all the spinach jokes aside. (It must be canned spinach that gave rise to all the put-downs.) There are different varieties, of course. The hardier varieties raised commercially and by large growers will probably have stems that are longer and leaves which are only slightly crinkly. Some small growers raise varieties which are very crinkly. These are more tender and fragile which explains why they aren't raised commercially. They also tend to have more flavor.

Season all year

Selecting

Spinach can be picked leaf by leaf as it grows but it will almost always come to market in complete plants since pulling the whole plant is a far speedier way to harvest than one leaf at a time. The outer leaves will be largest and inner leaves smallest. A number of plants will be bundled together.

The leaves should be perky and the color a healthy green. Darker green is more flavorful. Leaf size is irrelevant.

174

Using

When I was growing up, spinach was always served cooked. I don't remember it ever being eaten raw, but I think today it is used raw more often than cooked. I much prefer it that way.

Thoroughly wash the leaves to remove all sand and dirt. To use raw, add to tossed green salad or make the entire salad out of spinach.

When cooking, be sure to use the stems as well as the leaves. Some people find that the flavor of the stems resembles the flavor of asparagus. Cook just until tender. Be sure not to overcook or it will lose its delicious flavor and beautiful color.

CHARD

Chard is a large leafy green with individually harvested stems sold in bunches. Some varieties have creamy-colored stems and others have red stems. The leaves vary from slightly crinkly to very crinkly.

Season all year

Selecting

The leaves should have a fresh sprightly look and the stems should be crisp and unblemished.

Using

Unlike spinach, chard is always cooked. Wash thoroughly. Cut stems off and slice into bite-size chunks. The leaves can be left whole or cut into pieces. Put stems into cookpot with a small amount of water and cook for a minute or two, then add leaves and steam just until tender.

BEET GREENS

Beets are planted in rows, with more seeds being sown than the number of beets one actually wants to harvest. This means the plants must be thinned after they have grown awhile, and the home gardener has the luxury of eating tender young greens. He can also have slightly bigger greens with baby beets.

At the farmers' market, we aren't likely to find these very young shoots but we can, nevertheless, get delicious mature beet greens.

Season all year

Selecting

If you are especially interested in the greens you will pay less attention to the beets themselves and look for greens which are very fresh and as free as possible of creases and holes and other damage. Color should be rich. Wilted and yellowing leaves are not good. Smaller leaves will be more tender.

Using

Wash thoroughly and discard stems. Steam as you do spinach or chard. Or, if you want to serve the beets and greens together, use the following recipe.

RECIPE

Cooked Beets with Beet Greens

Cook the beets by themselves until tender, remove from pot to peel, put back into pot, add greens and steam approximately 5 minutes more until greens are tender.

Serve with wedges of ripe lime.

Metta Thomsen

TURNIP GREENS

Turnip greens have a slightly piquant flavor which makes them quite different from beet greens and chard.

Season fall and winter

Selecting and Using The same as for beet greens.

LEGUMES

The plants and fruits of this family are of great importance to man. They include alfalfa which is fed to cattle and used in organic farming to provide nitrogen in the soil. They include all the beans and peas we eat. They include the lupine which carpets the California landscape in glorious color during wildflower season and the wisteria which shades old-fashioned porches.

They provide us with lumber, dye, oils, proteins, resins, drugs, gums and honey.

The fruits are podlike which, when fully mature, split open into two halves. For this book we will be concerned only with the fruits found at the farmers' markets, peas and beans. (Botanically, they are fruits even though we refer to them as vegetables.)

Some, but not all, can be eaten in an immature state, meaning that we pick the fruit for the pod rather than the seeds. Sugar snap peas and green beans are examples.

They can all be eaten in their mature state, meaning that when the seeds inside the pod are fully grown we discard the shell and eat the seeds. Green peas and lima beans are examples. Full-sized seeds can also be dried if left on the vine long enough to start drying.

PEAS

There are two basic types of peas, those which must be shelled and those which are called edible pod peas.

Green Peas

I can remember sitting with my sister in the shade of a tree on an early summer day shelling peas freshly picked from our garden. Canned peas are pretty wretched things, in my estimation. (Home canned peas are abominable.) Frozen peas are acceptable. But nothing can compare to fresh peas. It is worth the work of shelling to have that wonderful taste and texture.

Green peas

Season late winter and spring

Selecting
Since you are eating the seed rather than the pod in this case, the pods should be plump and

the peas prominent to the touch. The pods should still be crisp and bright green.

If the pods are showing signs of drying out and feel limp or thin, they are over-mature for eating fresh.

Edible-Pod Peas

Also known as Chinese peas, there are two main types of these, the flat snow peas and the plump sugar snaps. There are many varieties of each kind so you will find varying sizes and shapes.

snow peas

Sugar snaps are a relatively new kind of pea, available for only about the last ten years. They look very much like the green pea which must be shelled, but the pod as well as the peas are eaten.

Season
Edible pod peas are a cool weather crop so are in abundance during winter and spring. But because of the differing climates around California and all the many varieties of edible-pod peas which have been developed, they are available almost year round at some of our markets.

Selecting
The pods must be crisp and should have a healthy color. Avoid pods which are blemished, an indication that they have been roughly handled or have been picked for some time. Appearance is important in this vegetable since it is used whole.

Using
Although new hybrids are being developed which are stringless, most varieties of edible pod peas have strings which must be removed. As you cut off the end, cut to the string and then pull down, pretty much a single movement. Turn the pea and do the same to the other end but cutting to the opposite side to remove the second end and string.

RECIPES

Flat snow peas can be eaten raw. They are most commonly used in stir frying where they are very lightly cooked.

Sugar snaps are used the same way, but because of their plumpness, they are a bit more versatile. In addition to munching on them raw and using them lightly cooked, you might want to try the following suggestions from Lori Nichols.

Sugar Snaps and Dip

For an hors d'oeuvre, prepare your favorite dips to accompany a bowl of fresh sugar snaps.

Stuffed Sugar Snaps

Split the pod open, remove the peas, mash them and add them to cream cheese or crab or any other filling you would like and then stuff the pod halves.

Frozen

Sugar snaps freeze very well. The blanching and freezing have the same effect as light cooking. When using them, they should be used in hot dishes where you normally use cooked peas. Do not cook them further. Add them at the last just to heat them. Frozen sugar snaps, because they are already cooked, are not satisfactory used as a substitute for raw peas.

SNAP BEANS

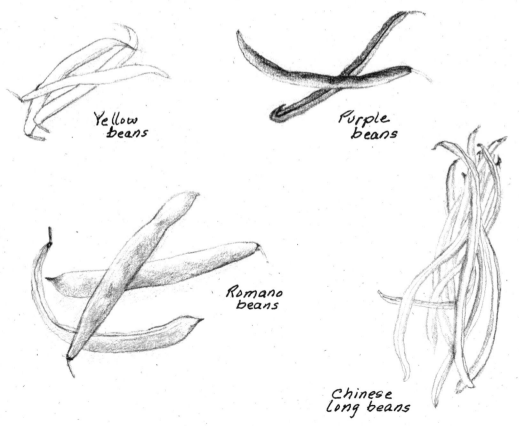

Yellow beans

Purple beans

Romano beans

Chinese long beans

These are edible pod beans which used to be called string beans for very good reason. They had fibrous "strings" along the edges which were inedible. New varieties have been developed over the years so that today the strings are often gone and there are far more varieties than ever before.

Standard green varieties include, among many others, Kentucky Wonder, Blue Lake, and broad Italian or Romano.

Haricots verts, or French green beans, are always very slender. They can be long or short, flat or cylindrical. They are more tender than other edible pod beans, and are considered a gourmet bean.

Yellow beans include the common wax bean and some newer varieties as well.

Purple beans look and taste like the standard green bean but have a lovely purple color. It's too bad they don't keep their beautiful color when cooked, but sadly they turn dark green.

Chinese long beans are slender green beans which reach more than a foot in length.

Fava beans are more commonly used in their mature state as shelled beans but can be used as an edible pod bean in their immature state when they are only 2-3" long.

Soybeans can be eaten in their immature state. There is a yellow variety, not the kind used for soybean oil, which can be used just like any green bean.

Selecting
Look for crispness. The fresher they are the crisper they are, and they will snap in half as soon as you start to bend them. The longer they have been picked, the more pliable they become.

Color is another guide. If beans are allowed to stay on the vine too long, the pod begins to lose its vigorous color.

Another thing to judge is the thickness of the pod in relation to the beans. Remember that with these beans you are eating the pod so it should be fleshy. In most varieties the seeds themselves won't bump up at all or only very slightly because they are very immature. There are a few varieties where the seeds are more prominent but the pod will be noticeably fleshy.

Season
Approximately late May through November.

SHELLED BEANS

All of the beans we have just talked about plus many more varieties can be eaten at their mature stage as shelled beans. There are numerous varieties with beautiful colors and patterns. Shelled beans are eaten fresh or dried.

Varieties for eating fresh
Following are the most readily available varieties at our farmers' markets.

Black eyed peas or Cowpeas Emi Tanioka likes the purple-podded variety best (the purple color should be deep). Other varieties can be more silvery or beige in color. She says that fresh-shelled black eyed peas are outstanding, much better than dried.

Cranberry beans (also known as Christmas beans) are bright red.

Fava beans (sometimes called horse beans or broad beans) are a very large bean. A word of caution regarding these beans: some people, usually of Mediterranean descent, may have a genetic trait which causes an allergic reaction to these beans.

Fava bean

Lima beans

Selecting
In this case, you are eating the seed rather than the pod so you are generally looking for the opposite qualities from those you look for in edible pod beans.

The pod is thin rather than fleshy, though still retaining some moisture. The exception to this is the fava bean whose pod remains quite fleshy.

The seeds inside should be large and well developed, and easily felt and seen through the pod.

Season Fall into winter.

Emi Tanioka's Fresh-shelled Black Eyed Peas

2 pounds peas

water

oil

garlic

onion

Shell peas. Place in cookpot with a small amount of water and oil, enough garlic and onion to flavor, and cook for just a few minutes.

You can vary this recipe by adding basil or tomatoes if desired. Emi says there is no need to use a ham hock to have wonderful black eyed peas.

DRIED BEANS

For using dried, the pods should be completely dry at harvest. You will most likely find dried beans already shelled and sold by the pound bag. Look for beans that are free of stones and stray seeds of other plants. They should also be free of mildewed beans which will appear much darker than the others and very likely be shrivelled as well.

I think you will find that the dried beans at our markets are of very good quality.

OKRA

Emi Tanioka of Merced comes from a family which has been farming in that region for over sixty years. When her parents came to the United States from Japan, they settled in the Central Valley where they purchased a small parcel of land. Her mother, Fude Tanioka, bought three heads of garlic at the grocery store and planted the cloves on her land. At harvest time she sold what she didn't need but kept more heads than she had started with to plant for the next year. Each year she saved more until she had enough to plant an entire acre.

Okra

Emi and her mother, now in her very late eighties, have been selling at the Merced market since it was opened in July 1980. "We haven't missed a Saturday morning in all that time - except for the seven month period when we couldn't get insurance for the market."

They raise many other vegetables in addition to garlic, including okra, and Emi was a great help to me on this vegetable as well as others. She and her mother have had as many as forty different items to sell on a given Saturday morning.

Okra is a green-podded vegetable commonly used in the southeastern part of the United States. Stew type recipes with okra added are called gumbo because of the thickening quality of the sap in the okra which is released with extended cooking.

Selecting
Spines or ribs: As in all fruits and vegetables, there are different varieties of okra and most have spines or ribs which should be tender when pushed gently. If the spines are hard, the okra is mature and will be too tough to eat. It needs to be picked twice a day during hot weather.

Length: The pods can be up to 6 inches in length if the spines are tender. The ideal size is 3 to 4 inches.

Scars: Okra is fragile and scars easily with handling. Look for pods which are free of scars, indicating it is fresh and has been handled carefully.

Color: Light green or reddish. The color should be consistent over the entire pod.

Storing
Place okra in the vegetable drawer of the refrigerator.

Using
Okra has the reputation of being slimy which prevents many of us from trying it. Emi Tanioka explains that it develops this trait only if it is cooked for a lengthy time. To avoid this problem, the secret is to add it at the last minute to a dish like gumbo, or fry just until the coating is brown.

Okra can be sliced and used raw in salad. It can also be pickled.

RECIPES

Emi says that among okra lovers, one of the favorite ways of eating it is breaded and fried.

Fried Okra

Okra

Cornmeal

Oil

Pour oil into heavy frypan and heat. Cut okra into 1/2" slices, roll in cornmeal, place in fry pan and stir until brown.

Emi Tanioka

Okra Tempura

Try dipping sliced okra in tempura batter for a change from the usual vegetables prepared this way. Be sure to remove from oil just as soon as batter is cooked.

Emi Tanioka

ONION FAMILY

ONIONS

There are many different varieties of onions which fall into two basic categories, early season and late season. Their colors are red, yellow, and white.

The early varieties, grown in mild climates while the days are still short, tend to be high in moisture and mild in flavor. Since they have a high moisture content, they have a short shelf life. They often have a flattened shape.

The varieties grown during longer and hotter summer days are more pungent and contain less moisture which makes them good keepers. They tend to be rounder in shape.

There are hybrids, of course, which mix the traits.

Selecting

Onions come to market both freshly pulled and dried. It used to be that almost all were freshly pulled, but as our markets have expanded and proliferated, the number of very large growers has increased and the predominant form is now dried. By dried, I mean that the outer layers of the onion have dried into the typical paper thin layers like those at the supermarket.

I have watched our local market evolve and feel a certain sense of loss as large commercial growers have taken over a larger and larger share of the market. Their produce looks too much like supermarket produce with commercial packaging. I like the freshly pulled onions. You can't get them at the supermarket. I like tomatoes to go out of season instead of having hothouse tomatoes to fill the gap. I like the one and two person operations where the grower is the person behind the stand and he can tell you how the weather affected his crop.

I also know that there are many trade-offs in this life and that those of us who are very small growers can't possibly meet the needs of the tremendous number of consumers who are looking for fresh produce at our markets. So we need these large growers and, even with their more commercial appearance, they and their employees are bringing the produce to you directly from their farms.

For my part, I will carry on the tradition of the true "backyard" grower and display my fruit in my collection of odd baskets and talk to my customers about pruning kiwi and how cold it was this morning when I went out to pick the blackberries.

Getting back to the matter of selecting onions, small growers will almost surely bring their onions freshly pulled. Large growers will most likely bring them dried.

Richard Wood, of Potter Valley, has given me helpful information about selecting and storing onions.

Size doesn't matter.

"Flatter is sweeter" is no longer valid because of the hybrids. It is the variety which determines the balance of sweetness and pungency. But Richard points out that weather, soil conditions, and cultural practices also affect the flavor and quality of any particular variety of onion.

To make selection easy, keep in mind the generalities - early, late, flattened, round, mild, pungent - and then learn the more subtle variations over the weeks as you shop. Ask the growers any questions you have and make notes right here on this page.

In any case, the onions you select should be firm all over. Look especially at the stem end for signs of spoilage and avoid any that have soft spots.

Storage

The early onions with their moist flesh can be held in a cool place in your kitchen for some weeks but will need cold storage to keep longer. Keep an eye out for the start of spoilage at the stem end, and if you see any, use the onion right away as the spoilage spreads quickly.

Green onions

The late onions can store in a cool place in your kitchen for six to eight months. If you purchase them with the skins already dry, they are ready for storage.

If you buy them freshly pulled in a quantity to store, you will need to be sure to dry the outer layers before storing so they won't spoil. For this purpose, the onions must be fully mature. That is, they will have a full round shape and the leaves will be quite dried out. Rest them single layer in a dry airy place until the outer layers of skin are paper-thin.

All onions can be picked at various stages of growth and have special names depending upon their growth.

Scallions are very young onions picked before the bulb takes on shape. The whole thing is edible though you will want to trim the roots off.

Green onions or Spring onions have been allowed to grow until a definite bulb shape has formed. They range from not much larger than scallion to golf ball size. Again, the leaves are edible as well as the underground bulb portion. The larger ones are excellent used whole in shish kebab.

Season - The scallions and spring onions start appearing in the market late winter and spring. The large onions appear in late spring through fall. It is unlikely that you will be able to get full size onions from February at the latest until the new crop appears in the spring.

SHALLOTS

shallots

Shallots are small bulbs made up of individual cloves. Plantings are started in autumn. When the leaves resemble chives, they can be harvested and sold at the market as a substitute for chives which are dormant at that time of year.

The shallots themselves are available late June through summer. They have a short shelf life so are best purchased fresh each week. Unfortunately, they do not dry or freeze well so they need to be enjoyed fresh during their short season.

GARLIC

Garlic is another bulb made up of individual cloves. It is planted in October and November, even into December. Some growers may bring garlic to the market in scallion form in the winter (February and March). Full size garlic will start appearing in May. It is a vegetable which needs long days to develop size so it is impossible to get good heads of garlic earlier in the season.

Garlic

The crop will be at its peak in June and July so this might be a good time to get a nice supply on hand. Quality will be high and the price will be at its lowest. It will continue to be available into the winter but it will be almost impossible to find any by late February. Garlic found in the supermarket from February to May comes from the southern hemisphere as it is out of season in California.

The garlic grower stops watering his crop about a month before harvesting which allows the leaves to dry somewhat. After pulling the bulbs, he lets them dry enough to pull the outer dirty layers of skin off. That explains the beautiful white color.

Sometimes you will see garlic that is just a little bit dark. This happens if rain falls or irrigation takes place in those last weeks before harvesting but the quality is not lessened.

To store garlic, the tops must be thoroughly dried first. Place them in an airy dry place away from the sun. Chances are that you will buy it already dry. Leaves are removed for individual garlic and left on for braiding. In a good **braid** the bulbs will not be touching one another.

ELEPHANT GARLIC

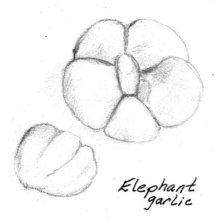

Elephant garlic

This variety of garlic acquired its name because of its size. It is almost always sold in clove form rather than in whole bulbs which can reach more than one pound in size.

The flavor is between that of regular white garlic and onions. It can be eaten raw but may be a little bitter this way. It is ideal for cooking (which removes any bitterness) and because of its size can be roasted just like potatoes and whole onions.

It keeps longer than regular garlic. It is harvested in early summer and, with cool dry conditions, can last until the following spring.

RECIPES
Elizabeth Krebs Roast Chicken

Stuff the cavity of a roasting chicken with apple quarters and elephant garlic cloves. The flavors permeate the chicken as it cooks for an excellent flavor.

Variation

My daughter, Catherine Wellington, offers this suggestion to accompany the above recipe. Squeeze the roasted garlic onto bread, spread, and eat along with the roast chicken.

LEEKS

Leeks are the mildest member of the onion family, looking very much like huge scallions. They can be slender to quite large in size, and the size does not affect quality.

Leeks

When selecting leeks, look for leaves which are flexible at the midway point, indicating tenderness. If the leaves are not flexible the leek will be woody. Also, check in the center of the leaves for a very round leaf resembling a stem which is a sign of over maturity and toughness.

To use, cut off the roots and wash. The entire lower white part is edible. Remove the dark green leaves as you move up the leek and use all the pale green to white interior.

Alice Pearce finds the dark green leaves excellent in many soups. They also add flavor to vegetable and meat broths.

Leeks are available all year.

CHIVES

Turn to Section IV and look under herbs for information on Chives, Garlic Leaves, and Shallot Leaves.

Chives
with flowering chive

NOTES

PEPPERS

Peppers, with their intriguing shapes, magnificent colors, and wonderful seasoning capabilities, attract the attention of food editors of probably every newspaper in the country. Therefore, the discussion here will be relatively short.

I spent time visiting with Elizabeth Krebs at her farm on a summer afternoon. She got her start in farming ten years ago as a migrant worker. This venture was followed by steady work for a local farmer. As she gained experience, she also gained confidence in her ability to run her own growing operation. Initially she was able to handle the workload herself but as her business grew she needed additional help. She now has two young women working for her.

"We're all women. It just happened this way," she says. What is it like with no men around the fields? All three agree they have an ideal working situation. They work together easily, not afraid to ask one another for help when the task at hand is too big for one. There is a strong spirit of cooperation and they all enjoy it. They enjoy the whole lifestyle, the farming, the fresh vegetables for eating, and their cottage in a very rural setting and yet only a block away from a main intersection in a small city.

Among all the other vegetables they raise are peppers.

Varieties
Basically, there are two kinds of peppers, sweet and hot. Most varieties fall into the latter group and vary from mildly hot to fire!

All peppers start out green and all turn a different color when ripe. This means that when you buy a green pepper of any type, you are getting an unripe pepper. Many peppers are used in their unripe green state. Others are much better when ripe.

Sweet peppers
Bell peppers are either red, orange, yellow, or dark purple when ripe and are much sweeter when ripe than while still green.

Pimentos are sweet peppers as well, and most people know them only as orange-red slices in little jars from the grocery store. Fresh red pimento peppers are perhaps the sweetest fresh pepper that you can eat.

There are also long, light yellow peppers which are mild and excellent for eating fresh.

Hot peppers
There are numerous varieties of these and it is hard to remember all their names so don't be bashful about asking the grower what varieties he has and how pungent

they are. They range from Anaheim and dried pasilla on the mildest side to fresh jalapeño and fresh habeñero on the hottest side. When ripe, colors include red, yellows of different shades and very dark purplish or blackish green.

Selecting

There are several things to look for, whatever the variety that meets your needs.

Any pepper should have a rich color and healthy appearance. Avoid any green peppers which have an anemic look.

Color and size are both important and related to one another. If you are going to use a pepper in its unripe state, it should not be too dark green for its variety or it will be immature. Ideally, a green pepper should be picked after it has achieved its full size but just before starting to turn color.

Avoid peppers with bad spots in them.

Plan on using the dark purple bell peppers raw since cooking causes them to lose their beautiful color just the way the dark purple beans do.

The best peppers appear at the height of the season. Those at the end of the season are not as good, even when they are allowed to get ripe.

Season

Summer and fall.

ROOTS AND TUBERS

I visited Metta Thomsen in her Santa Barbara home on a late summer day. We sat across from one another at her dining room table enjoying a cup of hot tea, while I asked her all kinds of questions.

Metta ran a school cafeteria in the Santa Barbara School District for 23 years before retiring. Now that she is no longer cooking for crowds of youngsters, she has more time to devote to her hobby of raising African violets. She has a special room where she raises hundreds of violets of every variety imaginable. She takes some each week to market and when I see a customer walk by, carrying a green berry basket holding a miniature African violet, I know he or she has discovered Metta's stand.

Metta's husband, Ernest, was in the construction business for almost 60 years. Together they grow many different fruits and vegetables, and glorious cut flowers in addition to the violets, which they sell at the farmers' market. They are very busy people! Among other things, we talked about turnips and carrots and beets.

BEETS

Beets are a straightforward vegetable. They come in different shapes ranging from round to elongated, resembling carrots. They also come in interesting colors. There are the common dark red beets like Detroit Dark Red which has been around since 1892. There are also pink beets like the Italian Chioggia and there are yellow beets.

Selecting
Size varies and is not important in selecting your vegetable. The beets should be firm and look fresh.

There is a difference in flavor among the different colored varieties so you may want to try the different kinds to find your favorite for day to day eating. My own is the good old-fashioned dark red which has the sweetest and richest flavor. The pink beets are next best and the yellow have the least interesting flavor. You may have a different preference, and even if you like the dark red best, there may well be times when you want the visual appeal of the contrasting colors.

It is best to select beets uniform in size so they will all cook in the same length of time. If you get a bunch with widely varying sizes, cut the larger ones so all the pieces you are cooking are approximately the same size.

Season all year

RECIPE
Hebe's Golden Beets

2 bunches golden beets with leaves

2 T rice wine vinegar

1 1/2 t honey

1 T butter

Wondra flour (or other thickener such as regular flour or cornstarch)

Wash beets and remove stems about 1 inch above beet tops. Cook in boiling water until tender. Dip in cold water. Slip skins and stems off.

Wash leaves thoroughly, discarding any that are yellow or badly damaged. Discard stems. Chop leaves, steam 2 minutes in water remaining on them from washing.

Add rice vinegar, honey, and butter to leaves. Cut beets into bite size pieces, add to leaves, and thicken with Wondra flour.

Hebe Bartz

BURDOCK OR GOBO

Until I started working on this book, I had no idea that there was an edible burdock. Burdock brings back memories to me of the days when I was a little girl and huge burdock plants grew wild out behind the barn. When the burrs grew to full size but were still green, my sister and I picked them to build doll furniture. They stuck together like today's velcro and we could pull our furniture apart to restyle it.

I also remember how bitter the burrs were! Why I would have put my fingers in my mouth which led to the discovery, I have no idea, but I guess we do a lot of things when we are seven and eight that we don't do when we are fifty seven and fifty eight.

The edible burdock found at our markets is, I am certain, a different variety. The Japanese call this vegetable gobo.

Emi Tanioka was a great help to me on this vegetable.

What to look for
It is the two to three-foot long slender root which is eaten. It is less tapered than a carrot and is brown on the outside. The end will probably be broken off on home grown roots as the root is so long that it is difficult to dig up the whole length.

194

Late summer into fall

Using

Burdock root has a rich earthy flavor. You will need to scrape off the outer layer, exposing the white flesh. Once this is done, you treat the root very much like a carrot.

From Emi come the following suggestions:

> Try grating some raw into a salad as an accent.
>
> Slice and add to soup
>
> Cut into shoestrings and add to stir fry
>
> Slice, dip into tempura batter and fry

If the center of the root is dry, simply cook longer. It provides good roughage.

CARROTS

Carrots seem to be limited to the color orange in slightly different shades. But they do come in a very interesting array of shapes and sizes. They can be long or short, skinny or fat. They may taper nicely to a point or they may remain quite constant in diameter and end in a flattened tip. They can be round like beets or radishes. Some are miniature and some are giant.

I learned from Leo Silveira, who has been farming in Santa Maria for fifteen years, that the same variety of carrot will vary in size depending upon the soil in which the vegetable is raised. Those grown in sandy soil can grow downward freely and will be thinner than the same variety grown in heavier soil. He believes those thinner ones are sweeter than the thicker ones.

Weather also affects the flavor of carrots.

Selecting

Most carrots sold at our farmers' markets have the tops on and they should look fresh and perky. Look for firm vegetables. They should not be soft or rubbery.

Size is a factor only as it relates to maturity. Mature carrots have full flavor. You must sacrifice this flavor if you want a baby vegetable since baby carrots are not miniatures but, rather, immature.

The little tiny rootlets on carrots are normal and easily come off with scrubbing. On fresh carrots these rootlets are very fine and not very noticeable. They grow larger and more numerous as the carrot ages, and since they are using the carrot as their food source, the carrot gradually loses its flavor and crispness.

I haven't seen any stored carrots being sold at the market but if you should buy in quantity and store them yourself, you may find these rootlets developing. Simply remove them before using.

Carrots which are not grown deep enough in the soil become green on the top portion. This greening affects the flavor and sweetness of that portion of the carrot so you might want to avoid getting these carrots, or, remove the green portion when preparing.

Beyond crispness and maturity there is no way I know of except trial and error to find the very best flavored carrots. Since they are so sensitive to soil conditions and weather, I find the best thing to do is sample until I find the flavor I like and stay with that grower until conditions change. Then back to sampling again.

Elizabeth Krebs recommends the Nantes carrot as one of the sweetest and tenderest carrots for eating fresh. There are other varieties which have more robust flavor for cooking.

Season
Carrots thrive in cooler weather so are more plentiful then. However, with so many variations in our California climate, many markets have carrots year round. Keep abreast of the growers and availability at your market so you can purchase in quantity if there will be a gap in production.

Storage
Put in the crisper drawer of your refrigerator after removing the tops. If you buy in large quantity to tide you over until carrots return to your market, place those that won't fit in your refrigerator in a container of sawdust, separating the bunch, in a very cool place.

JERUSALEM ARTICHOKES
(Sunchokes)

The name of this vegetable is a total misnomer! They are neither from Jerusalem nor are they artichokes. They actually are tubers from a plant in the sunflower family which is native to North America.

They are small brown to light brown tubers with bumps and protrusions. The interior is creamy white in color and crisp in texture. They have a mild pleasant flavor.

Selecting
Choose firm tubers with no green sunburn and no sprouting. Size is not a factor except as it pertains to your use. Smooth tubers with no protrusions are a bit easier to clean, but there is no difference in quality between them and those with protrusions.

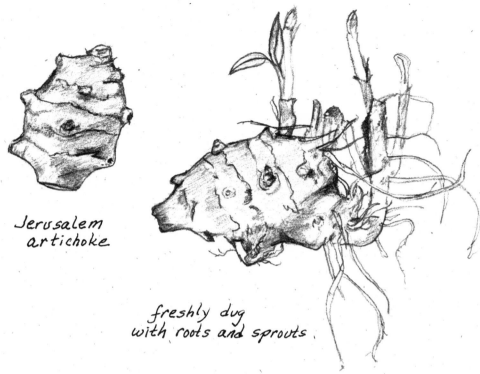

Jerusalem
artichoke

freshly dug
with roots and sprouts

Using

Chokes can be eaten raw or cooked many different ways. Scrub them thoroughly to remove all dirt and sand. They can be peeled but I prefer to leave the peel on. Raw, the peel is unnoticeable. Cooked, the peel remains rather crunchy while the interior is soft and I find the contrast of textures delightful.

Once cut, it will be many hours before the flesh darkens. However, if you wish to prepare a salad well in advance of company arriving, you might want to dip cut pieces in lemon or lime water to keep them at their best.

Note: Baked beans seem to cause flatulence in everyone. I have often wondered who thought up the tradition of baked beans and brown bread for Saturday night supper when we had to sit demurely in a church pew the next morning. Jerusalem artichokes are more selective than beans, causing a problem for only some people. If you are one of those, start out small and increase the amount you eat as your body adapts.

Storing

They can sit out in a cool room for a day or two. For up to a week of storage, leave in plastic bag and put in refrigerator.

RECIPES

Boiled Jerusalem Artichokes

Place peeled or unpeeled chokes in small amount of water and bring to boil. Simmer until tender, about 8 to 15 minutes depending upon size. If unpeeled, check for doneness through cut end rather than through skin since skin remains firm.

Sauteed Jerusalem Artichokes

Wash and slice thinly, leaving peel on. Put oil in fry pan, add choke slices and salt and pepper as desired. Saute just until chokes lose their raw white color or until nicely browned, whichever you prefer.

JICAMA

Jicama is a vegetable which has been commonly used in Mexico and Asia but little used here in the States. However, it is gaining popularity and growers are beginning to raise it for our farmers' markets.

Its shape bears some resemblance to turnips though it is usually much larger. The light brown skin has an earthen look. Inside is a crisp creamy-colored flesh whose mild flavor is compatible with numerous other vegetables and fruits.

Season Fall and winter

Selecting

Look for jicama which are free of blemishes.

Using

Always peel before using. It can be eaten raw or lightly cooked. It retains its shape and crunchiness even when cooked.

Raw, it makes a delightful nibbler when cut into strips. Use along with blanched broccoli, cauliflower, carrot and celery sticks with your favorite dips. Add to tossed salad.

It lends itself well to stir frying and skillet frying. Asians often use it as a substitute for water chestnuts.

POTATOES

Alice Pearce and her husband, Cloyd, are customers at the Santa Barbara Certified Farmers' Market and have been most helpful to me in the writing of this book. They have done extensive traveling and Alice shares the following information with us.

"Potatoes originated in South America, probably Peru. When we were traveling there, we met a man on the train who was a noted researcher of potatoes. He told us there are hundreds of varieties of potatoes grown in South America and they are important in the diet of the people there.

"In La Paz, Bolivia, we went to a farmers' market and saw huge numbers of piles of different kinds of potatoes covering an area at least twice the size of the Santa Barbara Saturday Farmers' Market."

As our farmers' markets in California proliferate and expand we are seeing more and more potatoes available. I am seeing some beautiful potatoes at the Santa Barbara market. They are so much better in quality than those at the supermarket that they are well worth the extra cost.

Varieties

There are many varieties of potatoes, and the ones at your particular market will vary from those at another market depending on the preference of the grower. The flesh will be white or yellow. Outer skin color will be pale tan to darker brown or it will be red.

Generally speaking, red-skinned potatoes, all white fleshed, are thinner skinned and are excellent for moist cooking methods. I find them at their best when cooked this way but there are people who like them baked so you may want to try them that way to find out your own personal preference. Some of the red varieties are Lasoda, Ruby, and Pontiac.

Tan-skinned, yellow fleshed varieties are also thin skinned and best cooked with moisture. They are very creamy. The most common variety is Yukon.

Tan and brown skinned, white fleshed varieties are numerous. Some are creamy and some are drier and more mealy. Traditionally, the mealier ones are the bakers. Freshly dug thinner skinned potatoes are best cooked with moisture. Those with thicker skins are excellent baked as well as cooked with moisture. As potatoes age, they develop more starch and this trait improves the quality for baking.

Some of the names you will hear are Burbank, Centennial Russet, White Tejon and you may even be told the variety you are selecting is known as A-57 or white ND. These refer to specific hybrids.

You might want to make note right here on this page of each variety you buy and how you best like it prepared. This will help you as the seasons bring different varieties.

Selecting

Potatoes can be damaged in the process of digging and you want to avoid potatoes which have gouges and cuts.

Potatoes which haven't been sufficiently covered with dirt during growth develop "sunburn" or green coloring. This is poisonous. It must be removed before eating and you can lose a fair amount of your potato in the process so you want to avoid getting potatoes with this problem.

Sprouts are an indication that the potato was picked quite some time ago and it is starting to grow again. Sprouts are poisonous and must be removed. However, the potatoes are perfectly edible once the sprouts are removed. If you store potatoes (see below under season) you will want to keep an eye on them, and remove sprouts as they develop to prevent the potato from being used as food for the sprouting new plants.

Size: Potatoes are equally good large or small so you should select the size that meets your use. The tiny ones are beautiful in vegetable platters or served with a parsley garnish. Baking potatoes should be larger, of course. Most people think baking potatoes should be enormous but I like to bake relatively small ones. They are done in a shorter time and fit the smaller appetite. Someone with a larger appetite can have two or three and even top each one differently.

Variety: Use will determine variety choice to some extent. See information above under varieties.

Season

There are two crops a year, spring/summer and fall/winter. If the grower has enough product and proper storage, it is possible for him to bring potatoes to market year round but it is more likely that there will be gaps in availability, especially late summer. To compensate for this, you can buy in quantity at the end of the season and do your own storage if you have the right conditions. Potatoes need a dark cool place, 40°, conditions not always easy to achieve in California where few people have cellars.

Sprout inhibitors are sometimes applied to potatoes. This is usually done by large commercial growers when shipping quantities of large potatoes. There is really no reason for a grower to do this on potatoes being brought directly to the consumer at the farmers' market but if you have concerns, especially at the end of the season of any particular variety, you can ask the grower whether he uses them.

RADISHES

Radishes are either very round or elongated like carrots. They come in shades of red, pink, purple, and white.

They are generally pungent though there are several varieties which are mild. Icicle, which is elongated, about 4"-6" in length, is a mild variety. The French Breakfast radish, also elongated, white topped and red at the tip, is very mild and recommended by Elizabeth Krebs for those who like a mild radish. The large white daikon can be quite mild if it is grown slowly in cooler weather.

Selecting
They should look fresh and be crisp. Some radishes become pithy when overgrown. However, you can't judge this quality strictly by size since size varies widely according to variety. You will need to depend on the grower for information on size and maturity of the particular varieties he raises.

Using
Most of us eat our radishes raw but some cultures use them in cooking. The daikon is perhaps the best radish for this use.

Season
Radishes, like the other root vegetables, thrive in cooler weather. This means they become scarce in mid to late summer but chances are that you will be able to find them pretty much year round. Those grown in hot weather grow rapidly and tend to be more spicy and are more prone to pithiness if not harvested soon enough.

SWEET POTATOES AND YAMS

To learn about sweet potatoes and yams, I talked to Joe De Ochoa of De Ochoa Farms in Selma. He is part of a small family farming operation which he took over from his father.

My husband and I, who have a very small operation, sell at only two local markets. I know the work involved for such a modest effort so I have great admiration for the growers like Joe who travel many miles to sell their produce at markets around the state.

"Yams" sold here in our country are actually a variety of sweet potato with moist deep colored flesh. "Sweet potatoes" are a drier, lighter fleshed variety. Yams usually have a dark red to purple skin and sweet potatoes have a lighter yellower skin. They both range in shape from roundish to oblong, often tapering somewhat more at one end than the other.

Season November into April

Selecting

Look for potatoes which are firm and as free of blemishes as possible. Avoid those which have been damaged in harvesting, or be sure that any damage is dry and healed to prevent spoilage.

Being a fruit grower and knowing only a minimal amount about raising vegetables, I was intrigued to learn from Joe that sweet potatoes must be cured after harvesting. They must be dried for three to four weeks in a warm (65°) place to prevent rotting. Be sure that the potatoes you are purchasing have been through this process.

Size is irrelevant except as it pertains to your use.

Storing

Store in a brown paper sack in a warm place.

TARO

Taro is a very interesting starchy tuber used frequently in Asian cooking. You will find it in two varieties at our markets, both of which are slightly mottled dark brown encircled with distinct rings. There is a large somewhat barrel-shaped variety which is less starchy and has a hint of turnip-like texture (though not turnip flavor). The smaller variety is much starchier and therefore, smoother in texture and somewhat dryer.

Selecting

Select firm specimens. The small variety may have little branches sprouting out from the sides which is fine.

Whether to get the large or small variety is strictly a matter of personal taste. Try both to find if you have a preference.

Using

Note: There is a substance in raw taro which can cause irritation to the skin of some people when they are peeling it. If you find you are one of these, simply put on rubber gloves or peel the vegetable easily after cooking.

Taro must be cooked. It is never eaten raw. Scrub the tubers well to remove dirt and fine rootlets. Peel before or after cooking, depending upon your use. You can boil, steam, or fry this vegetable. You can mash it or put it into soups and stews in pieces much like you do potatoes.

You can peel taro ahead of time since it doesn't turn brown with exposure to air. If you want to prepare well ahead of time, put in water to keep it from drying out.

The color will change from creamy white to grayish as it cooks and parts may even turn lavender. Water in which you boil taro will become a lovely pink.

I have read that taro must be eaten very hot because it becomes intolerably pasty as it cools. I do not find this to be the case at all.

Storage
Taro will keep nicely for an extended time in a cool dark place. Do not store in plastic bags.

RECIPES

Fried Taro - Quick & Easy

Peel and slice either variety of taro. Put small amount of oil in fry pan, heat, add taro and cook until taro is soft and gray. Season with salt and pepper if desired and serve hot.

I like to let the slices of taro cook until browned and somewhat crisp before serving. They are scrumptious this way.

TURNIPS

There seem to be few questions about turnips, a pretty straightforward vegetable. They can be egg shaped, top shaped, or round. They can be solid white or have purple on the upper half, all depending upon the particular variety.

Selecting
Size varies from small to quite large and is not important in selecting this vegetable unless it is extremely large at which point the turnip becomes pithy. They should be firm and look fresh.

As with beets, select bunches with uniform size turnips so they will cook nicely in the same amount of time. If they are uneven in size, cut the larger ones to match the size of the smaller ones.

Season fall and winter

NOTES

SQUASH & PUMPKINS

When a person starts a project such as this book, he has no idea of all the fascinating things he will learn. To make a decision about the placing of such things as luffa and chayote, I had to sort out some botanical puzzles which I think will intrigue you as much as they did me.

There is a family called Cucurbitaceae which is commonly known as cucumber family or gourd family. In this family are several genera, one of which is Sicyos where chayote belong. Another is Cucurbita where cucumbers, melons, squash, pumpkin, and gourds belong. This makes sense when you think about the structure of these fruits and vegetables. Chayote has a single seed and all the Cucurbita have numerous seeds.

Cucurbita is divided into several species, one for cucumbers, one for melons, one for gourds, and three where pumpkin, gourds and squash intermingle. At this point we learn that the commercially canned pumpkin one buys at the supermarket is actually squash.

For this book, I decided to group this family according to common use. Melons are covered in the fruit section. Look for cucumbers (most often used as a raw vegetable), edible gourds (used primarily in Asian cooking), and chayote (single seeded) under their own headings in this vegetable section. I have grouped all the squash and pumpkins together in this chapter.

To get some of my squash questions answered, I went to Barbie Graper who has been selling at the Santa Barbara Farmers' Market for many years now. She consistently has such high quality produce that a line starts forming more than half an hour before the selling bell rings. She is a one person operation and everything she sells is grown and handled with loving care. Her display reflects this joy of gardening and brings numerous compliments.

She taught elementary school for six years before "retiring" to become a farmer. Her love of gardening started with a flower garden when she was a girl and has continued ever since. She now has expanses of glorious flowers and rows of magnificent vegetables. I have had the pleasure of visiting her place in the foothills of Santa Barbara County and she has answered numerous questions for me for this book.

SUMMER SQUASH

We have what we call summer squash and what we call winter squash. You will notice that the varieties are different. In reality they can all be harvested and eaten in an immature state. They can all be grown to maturity and eaten at harvest or stored. But measured in terms of eating quality and storage, certain squash are better young (summer) and others better at maturity (winter).

Summer squash are picked at an early stage in their growth (immature), and the whole fruit is eaten, including seeds and skin.

A few of the Varieties:

Zucchini - long in shape, it can be very dark green all over, dark green with lighter green markings, also light green, or deep solid yellow.

Globe zucchini - round in shape, dark green with lighter stripes.

Yellow crookneck - large base narrows into a curved neck, light yellow.

Pattypan or scallop - a "flying saucer" with fluted edge, can be pale green, dark green, deep yellow or a blend of the latter two.

Other varieties can be straight-necked like the zucchini, round, or scalloped, and come in various shades of green, white and yellow.

Selecting

The size will not make a difference in the flavor but the smaller the fruit, the smaller and more tender the seeds will be. Look for a sheen on the surface. A young tender squash will be shiny. The bigger they are, the closer they are to maturity so look for a loss of this sheen in the larger ones.

Make sure the color is true to the variety. These vegetables are generally quite even in texture and color but there are two shortcomings to look for. Summer squash are susceptible to viruses which can create bumps or "warts" and can cause discoloration on yellow squash, giving them a mottled green and yellow pattern. They do not look as nice but they are fine for eating and the price should be lower.

The other shortcoming is damage in the form of nicks and bruises which are the result of hasty and careless handling. They spoil the appearance, and if the squash is not eaten in a few days, will tend to hasten the loss of quality.

Season

As their name implies, these squash are at their peak during the summer. They start arriving at the market as early as April and can be found as late as early fall.

Using

The flavor and texture vary slightly among the varieties so try each kind to find the one(s) you like best.

They may be eaten raw or cooked. To cook, drop cut squash into a small amount of boiling water or use a steamer. Do not overcook as it will lose its shape and fall to pieces.

RECIPES

Summer Squash Platter

Select a variety of very small squash with contrasting shapes and colors but similar in size. Steam whole and place in an artistic arrangement on a favorite platter.

Overcooked Summer Squash

If you get sidetracked from your cooking and discover your squash has become a limp mass that falls apart as you try to pick up individual pieces, take heart. Pour it into a colander to drain off the excess water. Then return to the cookpot, mash with fork or potato masher and add seasoning to suit your taste. A little butter and pepper makes this an excellent dish.

Baked Overgrown (Mature) Summer Squash

If you find yourself with a huge overgrown summer squash which is mature (the skin will be dull) and actually "ripe", you need not throw it away. Because the skin is sturdy and the seeds tough, these squash are excellent for stuffing. Choose a recipe from one of the cookbooks you already have or look in the appendix of this book for other cookbooks which would make excellent additions to your library.

Uncooked Summer Squash

Cut into cubes to add to salad.

Cut into strips for use with a dip or by themselves as nibblers.

SUMMER SQUASH BLOSSOMS

Zucchini provide the squash blossoms most commonly used for eating. The female blossom has a very small new fruit attached and is a California gourmet vegetable.

The male blossom looks identical but lacks the fruit and has only a very thin stem. This form is most used in Mexican cooking. In our markets both are available.

Selecting

Barbie Graper brings to market the most beautiful squash blossoms I have ever seen at our markets. She was able to give me excellent advice on selecting blossoms.

Blossoms can be purchased open or closed and it is very important to know what to look for. Blooms are open for less than one day only and open flowers are always a safe purchase. You can see exactly what you are getting. If you are getting female blossoms, it is best that they be open to assure that the squash has been fertilized, providing a firm fruit.

If you purchase closed blossoms the situation is more complex. Closed flowers must be picked just the day before opening. They should have a good strong yellow color, be very firm and shaped much like a carrot. If the closed flower is limp or soft or has a moist look to it, do not buy it. Those traits indicate the blossom was picked after it opened and had already closed again. Not only will it be inferior in quality but you may be surprised at what that blossom hides. The magnificent deep yellow flower, while it is open, attracts all kinds of little creatures such as flies, bees, cucumber beetles, aphids. As the flower closes up in the afternoon, some of these inhabitants are trapped inside. If the flower is picked and brought to market after it is closed, you may be getting some protein that you would prefer not to have!

RECIPES
Steamed Squash Blossoms

Using female blossoms, slit the baby squash lengthwise but not to the extent that it comes off the blossom. Stand upright in saucepan, using aluminum foil if necessary to support the blossoms. Using only a small amount of water, steam with lid on just until a toothpick indicates the squash is barely tender.

Barbie Graper

Sauteed Squash Blossoms

Steam blossoms as directed above. While they are steaming, melt butter in skillet and heat until slightly browned. Saute cooked blossoms briefly in this butter. Serve hot.

Barbie Graper

WINTER SQUASH

Winter squash are raised at the same time as summer squash but are left on the vine to mature so they are harvested later.

There are many varieties of all shapes, sizes and colors. I like to display a large collection of them in my kitchen throughout the fall and winter. My husband and I live in an old farmhouse from the early part of the century and since it is essentially unheated, produce keeps extremely well at "room temperature". If you live in a heated home, you can still enjoy a small display of squash. Cook the squash from your display and as you use it, replace it with new pieces brought from a very cool storage area. Use the squash first which has been longest in your heated room.

Now I'm going to take you back to botany and that genus Cucurbita. You don't really need to know all this but it is fun and can help you in picking out the winter squash that suits you best.

There are three basic species in this genus.

Cucurbita pepo includes many summer squash as well as acorn and spaghetti squash, and jack-o-lantern type pumpkins. These squash tend to be stringy in their mature or "winter" squash state, only slightly so in acorn and immensely so in spaghetti. They all have woody five-sided stems of substantial diameter.

This group tends to get stringier and lose sweetness with storage so is best used in the fall.

Cucurbita moschata includes butternut and Tahitian squash and the Dickenson Field "pumpkin" which is the variety most often used for commercial canning. These squash also have five-sided woody stems but they are much thinner in diameter than pepo, although they spread out just at the connection to the fruit. These are smooth sweet squash.

This group has the greatest durability and actually improves in quality with proper storage.

Cucurbita maxima includes Hubbard, banana, buttercup and turban squashes. These squash have round stems which are more pithy than woody. Their flesh is smooth, sweet and dry.

This group has excellent storing quality.

Selecting
All these squash should be heavy for their size and the skin should be dull. If the blossom end is showing signs of softness, the squash is beginning to dry out and should be used as soon as possible. Look for any wet soft spots on the surface which are the beginning of spoilage. If you should find such a spot after you get home, simply use the squash promptly, removing the bad area.

Size and color are not factors in judging quality. Color can vary on any given squash depending upon exposure to sun and contact with the earth on the underside.

Storing
Put in a cool area and try to spread them out so they don't touch each other.

Using

All of these squash are usually baked but can be peeled and boiled or steamed, and even eaten raw.

To bake: Leaving skin on, cut in half and scoop out all seeds. Bake as you do potatoes.

To boil or steam: Peel (butternut has only a thin skin which can be removed with a potato peeler but most other varieties have fairly thick skins which need to be removed with a knife). Remove seeds and cut into cubes. Place in steamer or small amount of boiling water and cook until tender.

The one exception to the above methods of winter squash preparation is the spaghetti squash. This variety is quite different from all the others. It is always best boiled rather than baked, and is cooked with the skin on. Small ones can be cooked whole, larger ones cut in half or quarters. After removing the seeds, the cooked pulp which resembles spaghetti is raked out. You can serve it with spaghetti sauce although you should keep in mind that it makes a substitute for spaghetti in much the same way as carob makes a substitute for chocolate.

To eat raw: Grate the solid portion in the neck of a butternut or Tahitian squash for use in a salad.

Freezing: If you find yourself with a squash which is just too big to eat in a couple meals, you can mash and freeze the cooked leftovers. It can then be later used as a vegetable or in pies and puddings.

PUMPKINS

Most of the information for pumpkins is just above in the winter squash section. Rely on the grower to let you know if his pumpkins are jack-o-lantern types which are inferior for eating or if they are excellent eating pumpkins.

TOMATILLOS

Tomatillos are a familiar sight in Mexico where they are used extensively. Here in the United States they have been a rarity until relatively recent years. Zeke Vargas of Santa Maria was one of the first farmers to raise this crop in California. He came with his family to this country from Mexico when he was fifteen. His father worked in the fields and Zeke followed in his father's footsteps. But after some time, he left the fields to became a licensed labor contractor, providing the workers for farmers. And finally, he became a farmer himself.

It was a natural for him to raise tomatillos, starting with one acre in Nipomo in 1975. He gradually increased his production to a peak of approximately 150 acres and was a major supplier to southern California.

He has since scaled back but continues to raise tomatillos, bringing them directly to the customers at our farmers' markets. He raises other vegetables as well for the farmers' market, and it was at the Goleta market that I had a chance to talk to him about this vegetable. He was a very willing and generous contributor of information for this book.

Tomatillos are round fruit hidden inside a papery husk. There are numerous varieties. The husks will be either pale green or purple. The fruit inside can be green, yellowish, creamy white, or purple, depending on variety and maturity. The size can range from very small like a tiny cherry tomato to as large as a small regular tomato.

They have a fresh, juicy, crisp texture, and a slightly acidic flavor, similar to green tomatoes and green peppers.

Season
Although tomatillos can be found all year at the supermarket where imported products are sold, they are available for only a part of the year at our farmers' markets. They will start appearing as early as May and last until frost or until the days become too cool and short for good growth.

Tomatillos

Selecting
The husks should be papery thin and dry. If the fruit has been picked too soon and is

immature, it will shrivel. The husk and a reliable grower are your best indications of maturity. The fruit inside will usually be green since that is the traditional way of using it. However, it can be creamy, pale yellow, or purple, depending on the variety and degree of maturity. Fully mature fruit will be sweeter and less acid.

Most often the husk will be very snug around the fruit and bursting open at the bottom. Sometimes the husk is much larger than the fruit. Either way is fine.

Using

Remove the husk and wash the sticky coating from the fruit. Although tomatillos are most often cooked, they are also very good raw.

Uncooked, you can slice them into salad, chop them up into fresh relish or puree into sauces and dressings.

Cooked, they are almost always used in some form of sauce rather than as a separate single vegetable. You can cook them for a few minutes by themselves very gently in a small amount of water before adding them to dishes. You can also roast them in a very hot oven, 450° to 500°, for about 15 minutes.

Storing

Tomatillos keep well. I have kept them on my kitchen counter for weeks in an open basket where air can circulate and keep the husks dry. They can also be stored in the refrigerator in an open container for several weeks. Do not store in a plastic bag where they will have a tendency to mold.

TOMATOES

Something I loved to do as a child was take two pieces of bread out to the garden where I made a vegetable sandwich on the spot with tomatoes, lettuce, onion and cucumber. I don't remember using any dressing, just those freshest of vegetables. I had a passion for tomatoes in particular.

In September, perhaps as late as October, my mother and father kept a close watch on the weather. The day would arrive when the first killing frost was expected that night. All seven of us would go out to the garden to harvest everything left above ground, including all the tomatoes that remained, even the green ones. This meant green tomatoes sliced, dipped in flour, and fried for dinner and if there were enough, my mother made more green tomato mincemeat, canning it for winter use.

Here in California the tomato growing season is much longer than it is in Vermont so I can enjoy them fresh for a much longer time. On the other hand, our tomatoes out here never seem to have the consistently rich flavor that northeast tomatoes have. Maybe they like summer downpours better than irrigation!

Varieties

There are many hybrid varieties today, developed for size, durability, and external appearance as well as resistance to disease. It is very likely that in striving for these characteristics, some of the flavor is sacrificed.

Colors are red, pink, and yellow. Size varies from the tiny cherry tomato to the very large beefsteak tomato. Round tomatoes come in all sizes, but oblong and pear shapes are found only in small to medium sized fruit.

Generally speaking, yellow tomatoes are lower in acid than red tomatoes. However, there are some new varieties of red which are lower acid as well. The grower can tell you about his particular varieties.

Some tomatoes have thicker walls and fewer seeds such as the pink beefsteak. The Italian oblong tomato has fewer seeds and is less juicy which makes it a good choice for sauce and paste where one wants to reduce the liquid through simmering. New hybrids have quite hollow interiors ideal for stuffing.

Selecting

Select tomatoes with rich color, deep red, strong pink, or deep yellow. The riper the tomato the stronger the color is.

While you may want large tomatoes for showy slices, consider getting tomatoes that are small for their particular variety as they seem to have more flavor concentrated in them.

Avoid any fruit with bruises or bad spots. Spoilage moves quite rapidly through tomatoes and you are likely to end up losing the whole fruit. If you find you have tomatoes with bad spots, remove the spoiled area completely. I rinse the tomato off and use my nose to tell me if I have gotten rid of all the spoilage. If you find a real bargain from some grower who has damaged fruit, there is no reason why you can't get the tomatoes. Just plan to use them right away for tomato preserves or salsa or tomato sauce.

Funny-shaped tomatoes can be fine but avoid any with pinhead sized dark dimples as they have earthy-tasting bad areas inside.

The best tomatoes are field grown and ripened. Those raised in greenhouses are very short on flavor but if they are vine-ripened they are at least juicy and soft and therefore far better than what I refer to as the "red rocks" that one gets at the supermarket in the winter. Those are actually tomatoes which were picked green and encouraged to turn red with ethylene gas. They certainly have the durability needed in supermarket merchandising!

Storing

The most important advice given to me by tomato growers is "Don't refrigerate tomatoes!" Simply leave them on your counter because chilling destroys some of their good flavor.

The ripest ones, of course, have the shortest shelf life so should be eaten first. Less ripe ones keep longer. Italian type keep longer as well because they have less juice. Tomatoes late in the season which are picked still somewhat green keep quite nicely. They will develop red color as they sit on your windowsill but will not improve much in flavor, which has to develop on the vine.

Season

Ten years ago we had tomatoes only in the summer and early fall at the market but now that our local market has grown to well over 100 growers who come from as far away as Fresno and Thermal, we have tomatoes year round. Different areas of the state have their peak tomato season at different times. Just as the hotter inland areas are finishing their field crops of tomatoes, the cooler coastal areas are coming into their peak.

In addition, there are now growers who raise hothouse tomatoes. This means that at the larger markets throughout the state, tomatoes are available in some form throughout the entire year.

MISCELLANEOUS

HERBS

An interesting discovery emerged from my research on herbs. The herbs that dry well can be grown year round in California. Those that don't dry well happen to be the ones that are seasonal. This means that, with few exceptions, you might just as well have all your herbs fresh.

Following is a list of herbs that I am aware are available at California farmers' markets and the months that they are available. Keep in mind that the availability depends on the climate in your part of the state and weather conditions. Also, remember that the supply will be greatest during the middle of the herb's season with shorter supplies at the beginning and end of the season.

Basil - spring and summer, into fall until first cool weather and rain storms. This herb needs longer days and warm temperatures for growth and is best fresh though it can be dried. It can also be frozen.

Bay - year round. If you come across bay leaves, you will want to determine whether they are the familiar bay of the supermarket or California bay. The familiar bay leaf is a slow-growing member of the laurel family and is mild in flavor. The California bay is an evergreen bush or tree native to coastal California and the lower Sierra Nevada elevations. It is a very pungent leaf.

Chamomile - winter and spring. It is the flower of this herb which we use. Dries well.

Chives - March through November at which time the plant starts going dormant. Does not dry successfully. Consider garlic chives and shallot leaves as substitutes in the winter.

Cilantro - year round. It is the fresh leaves you will find at our markets, but it is interesting to note that the seed of this plant is the familiar coriander.

Epazote - spring through fall. A Mexican herb which has become acclimated here in California as a weed/herb. It is purported to help remove the flatulence of beans. It has a strong flavor raw. B. D. Dautch describes it as resembling a sage/marjoram blend with a hint of pine.

Garlic Chives - winter. Interchangeable with chives.

Garlic Leaves - Bulb garlic grows slowly during the winter and the leaves are similar to chives so they can be used as a substitute for them. The leaves are a bit tougher than garlic chives.

Marjoram - year round though its slower growth habit in the winter causes less to be available at that season. Dries well.

Mint - There are a number of varieties grown mostly year round. This water-loving herb is at its lushest in late winter and spring when rains spur new growth. It is still attractive and available during the hotter and drier months. Can be dried but loses some flavor.

Oregano - year round though it grows more slowly during winter so there will be less available at that time. Dries well.

Parsley - year round. Both curly-leaved and Italian flat-leaved varieties are available.

Rosemary - abundant year round, dries well.

Savory - spring and summer primarily, though it can go into early fall. Loses flavor when dried.

Shallot Leaves - This vegetable grows nicely during the cool winter and the leaves can be a substitute for chives when they are out of season since the flavor is very similar.

Tarragon - March through fall. Loses flavor when dried. Sprigs can be preserved in vinegar.

Thyme - there are several varieties of this herb grown year round, though its growth is very slow during the winter. Dries well.

Extended season
It is possible for the season to be extended on these herbs if they are grown in a greenhouse. Occasionally there will be a grower who raises them this way.

Selecting
Look for perky leaves. Some of the leafier herbs such as mint can become droopy if they are sitting in the sun throughout the market. They will revive nicely once out of the sun if they were just picked the day of the market or the night before.

There are insects that love herbs and some growers control them with spray. You may want to ask how the grower raises his product.

Storage of fresh herbs
Be sure the herb is free of water (most herbs are sold in bunches which the grower keeps fresh throughout the market by keeping them in water). Place in a plastic bag, seal, and put in the warmest part of your refrigerator. The herb should last up to a week with this method.

Non edible herb

Lavender - I mention lavender because it is an herb sold at farmers' markets. However, it is not edible and is used for decorative and scenting purposes. Simply hang the bunches upside down to dry. When stems are dry (several weeks) they can be used as dry flowers, in potpourri, and in sachets.

RECIPES

A short time after we moved here to California, I started working for a paycheck. In return, my wonderful husband took over part of the domestic workload, specifically the cooking. He started out with hamburgers, boiled potatoes, frozen peas, spaghetti. As he gained confidence, he started experimenting and has become quite an excellent cook.

When he was selling at the market one summer, his neighbor was Michael Rouse who grows magnificent basil. They visited, of course, and Michael gave him the following recipe for spaghetti sauce developed by Greta Green. This and B.D.'s recipe are absolutely the best we have ever had.

Greta's and Michael's Spaghetti Sauce

1 c olive oil

6 cloves garlic, pressed

12 medium tomatoes, quartered

1 bunch basil, cut up

Saute garlic in olive oil. Add tomatoes and basil leaves. Simmer 40-60 minutes uncovered, stirring occasionally.

Serves 4

Michael Rouse
Greta Green

B.D. Dautch, who helped me immensely with this chapter on herbs, has his own variation of this recipe.

B.D.'s Spaghetti Sauce

Garlic cloves

Cherry tomatoes

Basil

Olive oil

Chop garlic cloves, cut tomatoes in half, cut up basil to size desired, and marinate in olive oil in the refrigerator for several hours. Use care in mixing to avoid damaging the tomatoes. Use uncooked.

B.D. didn't give me proportions. He recommends that you experiment with proportions to find the flavor emphasis that best suits your palate. He also explains that marinating mellows the flavors and people who normally don't care for raw garlic often like this recipe.

You might want to use B.D.'s sauce in the summer while tomatoes and basil are in season since it is uncooked. Greta's and Michael's recipe, being cooked, lends itself well to canning or freezing in quantity for the months when tomatoes and especially basil are not available.

Oregano

Sweet
Marjoram

Spearmint

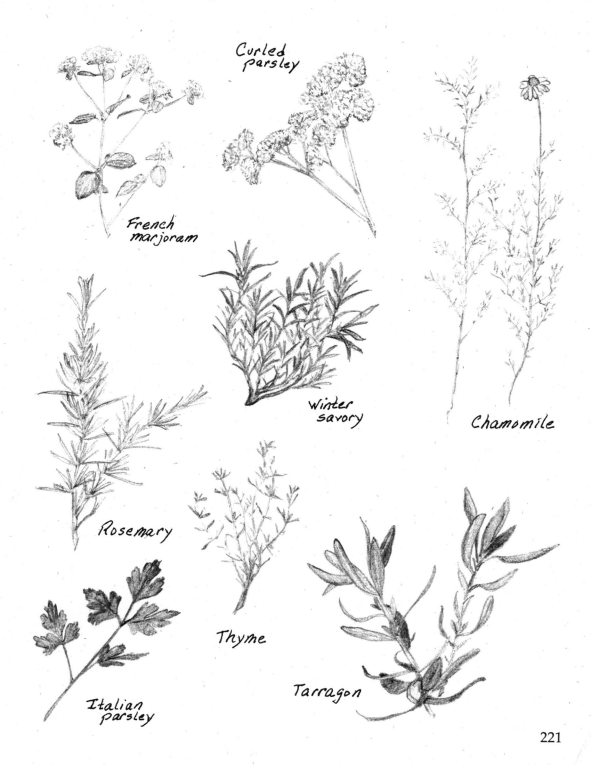

Curled parsley

French marjoram

Chamomile

Winter savory

Rosemary

Thyme

Italian parsley

Tarragon

221

NOTES

HONEY

Mark Sheridan is not only the manager of the Santa Barbara Farmers' Markets, he is also a beekeeper. He has been in the business for many years, and has been selling honey, honeycomb, and pollen at our markets. He is a soft-spoken, calm individual who is patient with all the growers and customers no matter what problem arises. I imagine these qualities which make him so easy to get along with in the human world make him easy to get along with in the bee world too.

It was natural for me to go to him for information on honey.

Honey is a sticky business literally, and figuratively, as well, when trying to answer customer questions, because questions and answers tend to overlap.

Forms
There are two basic forms of honey at our markets, extracted and comb.

Comb honey is the most natural and finest form. Not all beekeepers are able to produce this form because it requires special conditions to do so. It is made in the strongest hives with up to 60,000 bees which are forced into a smaller hive area to encourage them to store the honey rapidly.

When the comb is filled, the bees put a wax cap over the comb. There is an air space between the honey and cap which creates a white appearance in the honeycomb. The very finest comb honey is snow white.

Honey in this form has not been altered in any way, just portioned and placed in a container.

It is possible to get comb honey which has come from regular hive conditions but it will be inferior in quality. This honeycomb comes from the bees' living environment rather then a honey manufacturing environment. The wax is thicker, and the honey will contain particles of propolis, a resinous material which the bees gather from buds and use as cement. If the queen bee has used that part of the comb, the honey will have an off flavor. It will lack the lovely snow white appearance of the gourmet comb honey.

Drought years are not as good for this form of honey, so there will be less at the market.

With comb honey, one eats the comb and all.

Extracted honey is the other and more common variety. Extraction is achieved in two ways, one using centrifugal force and the other using filters, heat, and pressure.

Centrifugal force: A hot knife is used to slice the wax cap off the comb on both sides of the frame which is then put into an extractor and spun. Once the honey is drawn out and the comb is relatively dry, the comb is put back in a hive for the bees to start filling again. Since the wax is already drawn out into honeycomb shape, the bees have a head start on building up a new supply of honey.

The honey which has been extracted by this method is then put into a tank to settle. Since honey is dense, it sinks and any debris such as wax bits or wood bits from the hive rise to the top. The honey is drawn off into jars from a spigot at the bottom of the tank. The last bit of honey containing the debris is given back to the bees.

Filtering: In this method pumps are used to move the honey through a series of filters to remove debris. Since the honey is so thick, it needs to be heated to be liquid enough to pass through the filters. At the end of the filtering process the honey is put into jars.

The quality of the honey can be altered in this process. Honey is rich in vitamins and minerals which can be destroyed with the heat process. The summer temperature in a hive is about 100 degrees so temperatures above this in the processing can be detrimental.

Varieties

The variety of honey depends on the flowers from which the bees gather nectar. If the beekeeper places the hives in an avocado orchard when the trees are in bloom, the honey will be avocado. If the hives are in a clover field when it is in bloom, the honey will be clover.

Try different varieties when you shop because they can have quite distinctive flavors. Eucalyptus can taste like caramel and butterscotch. Orange is a classic California honey, quite aromatic. Wildflower is a blend of flavors. Avocado is a dark, rich honey with high mineral content.

Color

Honey varies from very light to very dark depending upon variety. Alfalfa honey is light and avocado is darkest, next to buckwheat. The darker color honey has more nutritional value because the color comes from minerals in the nectar. There is also what is known as bakery grade honey, and this is the one exception to the relationship of color to nutrition. This grade of honey is very dark from overheating, not from minerals.

Grade

Honey is graded by water content and color. To make honey, bees draw the water out of the nectar which they collect. The beekeeper uses a meter to measure the water content to assure that it is low enough.

Color ranges from white through various shades of amber. Grade A honey has a beautiful appearance, and when you want an exceptionally light clear honey, use this. However, Grade A is actually the most filtered and heated honey, so from a nutritional standpoint it does not stand up to US Standard Grade C honey which is unheated and allowed to settle.

Crystallized Honey

All honeys can crystallize but winter honeys, especially eucalyptus, are very prone to this change. Crystallization is normal and there is nothing wrong with this honey except that it won't pour. Different varieties have different sized crystals. If your honey should crystallize, you can warm it to return it to a liquid state. Keep in mind that a slow gentle warming will keep the vitamins intact, whereas a less patient burst of higher heat will reduce the quality.

Mark solves the crystal problem by making spun or creamed honey, a process which whips air into the honey and breaks the crystals.

Other Information

If you see bubbles at the shoulder of a jar of honey, do not buy it. Bubbles mean the honey is "green" and fermented because it was extracted before the sugar content was high enough. Bees do not cap the cells until the sugar content is up to 17% so any honey extracted before capping is too low in sugar content.

Storage

Honey is hygroscopic, which means it takes moisture and flavors from the air. Since you want it to remain thick and low-moistured, honey should be kept covered. It also is a magnet for odors. In fact, one cigarette in the extracting house can ruin a whole batch of honey.

BEE POLLEN

Bee pollen is the protein food for the growing young in the bee colony. The bees collect it on their legs as they are gathering nectar, and the colors vary depending on the particular type of flowers the bees are visiting.

The beekeeper puts a series of screens at the hive entrance which does not cause any harm to the bees but does remove the pollen from their legs. A small entrance is left free so ample protein can be taken to the young.

The pollen is high in amino acids, and is used by some people as a nutritional supplement.

MUSHROOMS

David Mountain gave me a fascinating tour of the exotic mushroom business which he and his wife run in the Santa Barbara area. He took me first to their lab, complete with gleaming glass test tubes, where Susan clones existing mushrooms. She starts the growth of the mycelia (which can be thought of as a root system) in agar, a liquid medium, then adds bran to the liquid to nourish the growth. Following two weeks of growth, the mycelia are chilled for forty-eight hours.

The next step in the growth process is transferring the mycelia to bags of sterilized moist straw in which they are incubated in the dark until they reach the appropriate stage for "transplanting" to a compressed sawdust medium. (An interesting little note - David says they get their hardwood sawdust from a skateboard company.) The compressed sawdust simulates the bark and fallen trees which would be the natural place of growth for mushrooms.

When we moved on to the room where the final stage of growth takes place, I was greeted by the kind of cool misty air one finds in the forest in the early morning, and the light was soft as if coming through a canopy of trees. David and Susan try to duplicate the natural environment of mushrooms as much as possible by regulating the temperature, light and humidity, varying each throughout the day and night.

David showed me some newly-emerging mushrooms on one of the compressed blocks. They blended in so nicely with the growing medium that I never would have known they were mushrooms had he not told me.

I had no trouble recognizing the mushrooms ready for harvesting for the next day's market. Shiitake were already resting in one of the wicker tray baskets the Mountains use to display their product.

Some mushrooms can be started under laboratory conditions but then must be placed in the natural environment to complete their growth. There is a symbiotic relationship between the fungus and the host. Chanterelle is one of these. The mycelium can be encouraged to grow in the lab but it won't fruit, so needs to be placed in an oak forest. The Mountains lease land in another county for this mushroom. By "planting" the mycelium, they can greatly increase the size of harvest. Susan refers to this as forest management.

David says they are always experimenting with new methods of growing. One of those is placing the mushroom spore in holes drilled in short logs. The holes are sealed with paraffin and it will take up to a year before there is any sign of growth. The idea here is to more accurately duplicate the mushrooms' natural environment. The resulting mushrooms are much heartier in flavor than the cultivated mushrooms.

This idea of experimenting seems to be common among growers. We feel close to the earth and nature and have the sense of nurturing living things. We also have limitless opportunities for experimenting. It may be duplicating the natural environment as the Mountains do. It may be figuring out how to outsmart the flea beetles that make lacework of our arugula leaves. Or it may be trying a new fruit tree that few people have heard of. Could it be the next kiwi or cherimoya?

Following are some of the varieties of mushrooms to look for at your farmers' market.

Common white button mushroom Since this is so familiar there is no need to elaborate here but it is perhaps the most readily available mushroom variety at our farmers' markets.

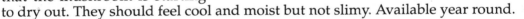

Oyster mushroom This mushroom, which has the blue-gray color of oysters when young, starts to turn brown as it ages. It grows in the form of many plates around a "stem", giving a layered appearance.

Size does not affect flavor but smaller ones will be more tender and larger ones meatier. They should be springy. There should be no yellowish-brown ridges on edges which indicate that the mushroom is starting to dry out. They should feel cool and moist but not slimy. Available year round.

Shiitake

Use just as you do the common button mushroom, fresh in salad, sauteed to accompany meat or vegetables, or cooked in your favorite pasta sauce.

Shiitake This mushroom has a beautiful warm brown color on the top of its rather large flat cap. Look for a firm cap with white gills. If the edges of the cap curl under, it is considered more prized. Available year round.

This mushroom is best cooked. Saute on high heat for 2-3 minutes.

Chanterelle This mushroom is deep yellow in color. Its thin cap starts to turn upward with a rippling effect, leaving the center depressed.

This is one of the mushrooms which can be started in the lab but must be "transplanted" to its natural environment. That means it is available only from late summer through December. It can be available as late as March if the season is wet. The remainder of the year it is available only in dried form.

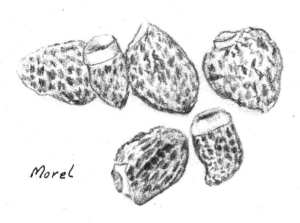

Morel

Select mushrooms with no wet brown spots, no sweating or slime. They should have a pumpkin apricot fragrance.

Morel In shape this mushroom resembles a pine cone on a short fat stem. The surface looks a bit like coral or sponge. It grows in the wild and must be gathered through spring and into June. The remainder of the year it is available dried. Blonde morel is found in orchards and meadows. Black morel is found in disturbed forest or burn areas.

David says this mushroom is prized by chefs *and* worms! Look for these little creatures when selecting. This mushroom is soft and should always be cooked.

Coral This mushroom is creamy white and looks very much like a round piece of coral. When selecting, look for mushrooms which have no brown spots. They should be spongy but no moisture should come out when they are squeezed. They are available year round.

They are best cooked a short time. Because they are solid roundish balls, they are very versatile. Small whole ones lend themselves very well to shish kebab. They can be barbecued, broiled, baked or sauteed.

If you eat them raw they shouldn't be bitter. Bitterness is a sign of age.

A delicious and simple way to prepare them is suggested by David Mountain. Brush them with garlic, oil, and lemon juice. Bake or saute. Add parmesan cheese as well if you like.

Porcini The name means "little pig" in Italian. The French name for this mushroom is "Cepe". In reality, the variety we find at our farmers' markets is not the Italian variety from which it derives its name, but a California mushroom.

Look for large firm dry specimens when selecting. Worms are even fonder of this mushroom than they are of morel, so keep an eye out for them.

This mushroom has a rich beefy flavor and should always be cooked. It is especially good in pasta and risotto.

Storing

Keep mushrooms in a closed paper bag in your refrigerator. They like a cool dark moist environment. However, never wash mushrooms until just before using them as water sitting directly on them will cause them to spoil quickly.

SPROUTS

I can remember when our market was still small, a mere handful of growers with not much of any one commodity. As we expanded, we experienced growing pains. I was the only one with lemons, selling large quantities at 10c each and one day another grower came in with lemons. My sales slowed for a time but the added growers attracted more customers and in not too long a time, my sales were back up where they had been.

I recall this experience because at one time we had two regular sprout sellers. As others came in, the second of the two original sellers approached the board of directors and requested that the market limit the sprout growers to just the original two. She felt she had unfair competition. The board very wisely did not grant her wish. Consequently, the market continued to expand until today every grower spot is full and the aisles are crowded with shoppers.

We now have a number of sprout growers and we need them all to fill the demand. Thank goodness there are other lemon sellers. I couldn't possibly meet the needs of all the customers we have today!

Sprouts can be grouped into three different categories, all of which are available year round.

Sprouted seeds In this case the seeds are just barely sprouted and you are eating the seeds themselves.

Sprouts of dicotyledons The veins in the leaves of these sprouts are branched. This group includes most of the sprouts we eat in leafy form.

Wheatgrass, a monocotyledon The veins in the leaves are parallel. This grass is used in leafy form to make juice.

Sprouted Seeds

Sunflower seeds are gray and moist with just the very smallest bit of sprout projecting from the end.

Storing
They will keep for up to one and a half weeks if you rinse them every few days and keep them stored in the refrigerator in a plastic bag. Remove the portion you want to use and return the rest to the refrigerator.

Using
They are eaten raw and make an excellent addition to a tossed salad. Try adding them to cooked rice or soup. You can put them in the dough when making a hearty

yeast bread. I tried them in my old fashioned oats for breakfast one morning and decided that was not the way to eat them. But that doesn't mean you shouldn't try that idea if it appeals to you. (After all, I don't like cheese with my apple pie either!)

Other varieties seem to be limited only by the imagination and energy of the grower. There are sprouted soybeans, peas, radish, mustard and more.

Mixtures of sprouted seeds are common and can come in mild or spicy versions. The mix varies from grower to grower so you can ask him questions and try different mixes.

Except for the sunflower, these sprouted seeds all have a distinctly raw flavor.

Storage and Use
They can be stored the same way as sunflower seeds and are used primarily in salads. You can also add them to cooked rice and soups.

Leafy Sprouts

While sprouted seeds require only about two days growth before they are ready to eat, the leafy sprouts may take up to as much as three weeks before they are ready.

Alfalfa and clover are raised in soil but all others are raised with compost. The seedlings need misting, ranging from as often as eight times a day to only once every two to three days.

Selecting
With the exception of pea, the sprouts should have only the initial two leaves. In the case of the pea, there will be several sets of leaves but they will not be fully opened. A taste test (with permission of the grower) can let you know the quality. Avoid bitter or soft sprouts.

Using
These sprouts are all used fresh and uncooked in salads and sandwiches.

Storing
These sprouts are best stored in the refrigerator in the plastic bag in which you get them at the market. Avoid excessive moisture which can make them spoil more quickly.

Common Varieties
Alaskan Pea tastes very much like raw peas.
Alfalfa and Clover
Buckwheat
Daikon Radish is spicy, good added to stir fry at the last minute.
Fenugreek
Sunflower is excellent for eating plain as a snack.

Wheatgrass

This sprout is quite different from other sprouts in that it is used almost exclusively for juice. Since the leaves are very fibrous they are not satisfactory in a salad or sandwich, a bit like eating old-fashioned string beans from which the strings haven't been removed.

The best way to use these sprouts is to extract the juice with a wheatgrass juicer. The juice is strong and sweet and must be consumed when freshly squeezed as the sweetness is rapidly lost.

Some people believe that the chlorophyll in wheatgrass juice is a blood tonic which cleanses the body. This sprout is usually purchased by the flat rather than by the half pound or pound, since it is squeezed rather than used as a green.

NOTES

Other Sources of Information

GENERAL INFORMATION

Agricultural Commissioner's Office

Look in the white County Government pages of your phone book. This office can give you information on local farmers' markets.

Cooperative Extension - University of California

Look in the white County Government pages of your phone book. This office can provide recipes, information on drying and preserving, and answer questions on food safety.

The Date Palm, Bread of the Desert
Hilda Simon
1978, Dodd, Mead & Co.

Out of print. Check second hand bookstores and the library.

Farmers Markets of America, A Renaissance
Robert Sommer
Capra Press

Out of print. Check second hand bookstores and the library.

Fresh Produce A to Z, How to Select, Store & Prepare. Over 250 Recipes
By the Editors of Sunset Books
Lane Publishing Company
Menlo Park, CA 94025
1987 $7.95

I highly recommend as a companion to this book.

The Greengrocer
Joe Carcione

Out of Print. Check second hand bookstores and the library.

Small Farm Center
University of California
Davis, CA 95616-8699
Tel (916) 757-8579

Information about certified markets throughout the state of California as well as information about farm stands and U-pick operations.

Uncommon Fruits and Vegetables, A Commonsense Guide. Over 400 Recipes.
Elizabeth Schneider
Harper & Row, Publishers,Inc.
$16.95

I highly recommend as a companion to this book.

U-Pick, U-Profit, Direct-Farm Marketing for the Consumer
Diana Burnell
Berry Fine Publishing Company
Post Office Box 457
Aumsville, Oregon 97325
1982 $6.95

Your Desert and Mine
Nina Paul Shumway
1979, ETC Publications

A story of date horticulture and Coachella Valley in the early part of this century.

NUTRITION AND FOOD SAFETY

Agricultural Commissioner's Office

See under General Information.

Composition of Foods
Agriculture Handbook No. 8
Superintendent of Documents
U.S. Government Printing Office
Washington, D.C. 20402
Stock no. 001-000-00768-8
Catalog no. A1.76:8/963

A 190 pg publication with extensive information on the composition of foods and nutritional details.

Cooperative Extension - University of California
See under General Information.

Issues in Food Safety
Quarterly newsletter published by The Fresh Produce Council and the Alliance for Food and Fiber. For copies, contact:
Fresh Produce Council
1601 E. Olympic Blvd., Suite 212
Los Angeles, CA 90021
(213) 629-4171

The spring 1989, Issue 2 of Vol. 2 is especially helpful in understanding the food safety concerns touched on in Chapter 5 of this book.

PRESERVING, DRYING & DEHYDRATORS

Ball Blue Book, 32nd edition
Home canning book put out by Ball Corporation
To order, send $3.50 (includes shipping) to:
Direct Marketing - Dept. GL-1
Ball Corporation
P.O. Box 2005
Muncie, IN 47307

The Complete Food Preservation Book
Beverly Barbour
McKay Company, Inc.

> *Includes directions for making solar drier. Out of print. Check second hand bookstores and the library.*

The Dehydrator Cookbook
Joanna White
Nitty Gritty Cookbooks
1992 $8.95

Fruit Drying With a Microwave
Isabel Webb
Sterling Publishing Co.
1992 $8.95

Kerr Kitchen Cookbook

> *Home canning and freezing book put out by Kerr*

To order, send $3.50 plus .50 shipping & handling per copy to:
> Kerr
> Dept. CL
> P.O. Box 76961
> Los Angeles, CA 90076

Putting Food By
Hertzberg, Vaughan, & Greene
The Stephen Greene Press

> *Includes directions for making trays and driers.*

Sunset Home Canning, Preserving, Freezing, Drying, Pickling.
By the Editors of Sunset Books
Lane Publishing Company
Menlo Park, CA 94025
1993 $8.99

COOKBOOKS

The Avocado Lovers' Cookbook
Joyce Carlisle
1985
To order, send $9.95 plus $1.50 postage and handling for each copy to:
> Blue Ribbon Publishers
> 5587 W. Camino Cielo
> Santa Barbara, CA 93105

Buy it Fresh Cookbook
A project of the American Friends Service Committee
Heart of the City Farmers' Market
111 Golden Gate Ave.
San Francisco, CA 94102

Creative Squash Cookery
Mary Mazzia
1982
Available at the Serra Shop, Old Mission, Santa Barbara
> or

To order, send $4.95 plus $1.00 postage and handling for each copy to:
> Mary Mazzia
> 2030 Las Canoas Road, Dept. L
> Santa Barbara, CA 93105

The Farmers Market Cookbook
City of Alhambra Certified Farmers Market
City of Alhambra
Department of Human Services
111 S. First Street
Alhambra, CA 91801

The Fresh Farmer Cookbook
The Torrance Certified Farmers' Market & The Torrance Historical Society
City of Torrance Parks & Recreation Dept.
3031 Torrance Blvd.
Torrance, CA 90503

Garden Sass, A collection of recipes by the growing seasons
Compiled by the Barn Browsers, The Fort at #4, Charlestown, NH
To order, send $9.95 per copy plus $2.40 postage and handling for first copy and 60c
for each additional copy to:

                  Old Fort No. 4 Associates, Inc.
                  P.O. Box 336
                  Charlestown, NH 03603
Allow 4 weeks for delivery.

The Garlic Lovers' Cookbook, Vol.II
From Gilroy, the Garlic Capitol of the World
Celestial Arts
Berkeley, CA
1985 $9.95

GENERAL INDEX

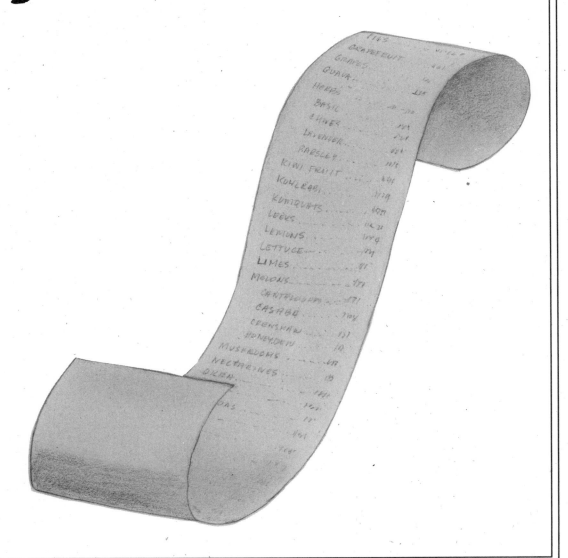

GENERAL INDEX

RECIPE INDEX

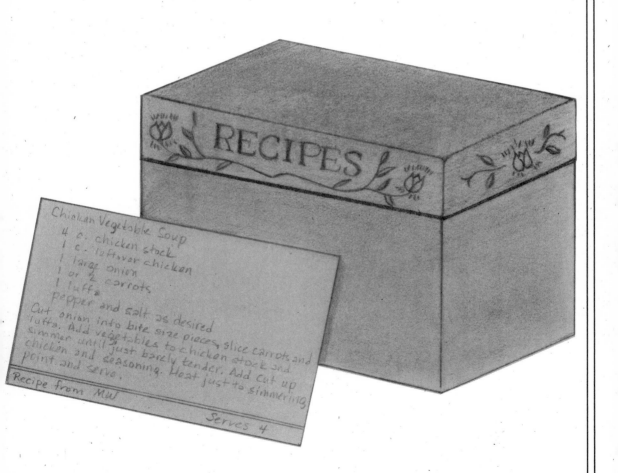

Chicken Vegetable Soup
4 c. chicken stock
1 c. leftover chicken
1 large onion
1 or 2 carrots
1 luffa
pepper and salt as desired
Cut onion into bite size pieces, slice carrots and
luffa. Add vegetables to chicken stock and
simmer until just barely tender. Add cut up
chicken and seasoning. Heat just to simmering
point and serve.

Recipe from MW

Serves 4

RECIPE INDEX

Order Form

_____ copies of Limes Are Yellow @ $15.95 each $_____

shipping and handling @ $1.00 each   _____

CA residents add $1.24 tax each   _____

Total enclosed $_____

Send to:

     Limes Are Yellow
     Sorrel Publishing
     P.O. Box 2492
     Santa Barbara, CA 93118

Be sure to include your name and address. Allow 4 weeks for delivery.

Order Form

_____ copies of Limes Are Yellow @ $15.95 each $_____

shipping and handling @ $1.00 each   _____

CA residents add $1.24 tax each   _____

Total enclosed $_____

Send to:

     Limes Are Yellow
     Sorrel Publishing
     P.O. Box 2492
     Santa Barbara, CA 93118

Be sure to include your name and address. Allow 4 weeks for delivery.